TASTY EXPRESS

SNEH ROY

TASTY EXPRESS

SIMPLE, STYLISH & DELICIOUS DISHES FOR PEOPLE ON THE GO

EBURY PRESS

For Nicky, Rivan & Rish
You make me who I am
I love you
X

CONTENTS

WELCOME
TO TASTY EXPRESS

One of my earliest memories of food is kneading dough on my mother's kitchen table with stormy grey skies outside and the rain pelting down on the windows. To this day, the smell of bread makes me inhale a deep breath of contentment and all I can smell is the beautiful aroma of the first raindrops on rich soil. Food has that power: to capture a snapshot in time of a poignant memory and replay it for you when you need it most. It is truly a celebration of all the senses.

I was born in India and grew up in bustling Mumbai when it was called Bombay. It was a fantastical place, forever festooned with crowds, colours, flavours and culture. I grew up on some of the best street food the country has to offer.

A couple of decades later I married Nick, my college sweetheart, and we moved to Singapore. There we immersed ourselves in the culinary delights of South East Asia, from Malaysia to Thailand and everything in-between. When I finished my day working as a designer and web consultant, I would spend my night cooking and nurturing a food blog.

Cook Republic started as a small online cooking journal in 2005 and grew into a visual timeline of my food adventures and daily life when we moved to Australia. Nearly eight years after its conception, it won Best Blog in the Australian Writers' Centre Best Australian Blogs awards in 2013. The overwhelming love and support from the online community and people in the real world touched me to the core.

We now call Sydney home where we live with our two boys, two rabbits and four crazy chooks. We used to have a garden full of veggies, but that was before we welcomed the chooks (darned chickens!). Our life in Sydney is constantly busy and varied. We love daily chicken chasing, weekend fruit picking at local orchards, weekly visits to farmers' markets, scouring the local nurseries for that new herb pot, packing picnics for bike rides, and cooking together. Kneading bread and making fresh pasta dough with the boys is one of our favourite activities, one that often ends up with too much flour on the floor and a lop-sided loaf. Because we are always on the go, the food I have created for this book reflects my commitment to developing fast, simple, tasty and wholesome dishes for the whole family.

I am not a trained chef, merely an enthusiastic cook who is always hungry for more. My style of cooking is adventurous and fun and I love creating easy twists on time-tested classics. I have always been a champion of fresh, reasonably fast and exciting food – the kind of dishes that lead a double life, happily going from a hard working lunchbox staple to an exciting dinner side or lazy weekend breakfast. Very often a good knife, a pan and a handful of fresh ingredients is all you need. This has always been my kitchen mantra.

In *Tasty Express* I share with you some of my dearest recipes from my childhood in India – with a modern makeover, of course. I also share recipes that have been inspired by the countless market stalls, food trucks and famous eateries I have explored in all the countries I have visited or lived in. And there are plenty of naughty treats because we all need one!

Because I mainly eat a plant-based diet, the recipes are predominantly vegetarian, but they can easily be adapted to include your own preferences. For example, Sweet & Sour Potatoes could easily be transformed with pork or chicken, a quick stir fry like Spicy Moroccan Sprouts would welcome the addition of fresh tiger prawns, the Cashew & Pea Curry could be made heartier with succulent pieces of lamb and the scrumptious Beetroot Leaf Flatbreads could be bumped up with mince. The occasional meat dish makes an appearance every now and then, and likewise most of these can be adapted to suit vegetarians. Nick's Minced Lamb Tacos would be equally delicious with finely chopped mushrooms and the prawns in the Tea Smoked Fried Rice could be substituted with chunks of firm marinated tofu. The recipes are flexible and the possibilities to make them your own are endless.

I reveal recipes that will enhance your cooking experience because they are so ridiculously easy, like a luscious One-Minute Coconut Mug cake with Creamy Lemon Curd to keep you company on the couch at night, or a delicious cup of hot chocolate spiked with chai to warm your breath on a cold morning. I show you a never-fail method of cooking quinoa because having a box of cooked quinoa in your freezer will change your life! I show you how to grow sprouts with every imaginable legume and seed on your kitchen counter using just a jar and a piece of paper towel. I bring you breads that go from flour to loaf in under one hour, five-minute chutneys you could take along to barbecues, nutrition-dense muffins that freeze well and cheeky granolas you could package for Christmas gifts. Plus there are heaps of sauces, smoothies, dips, cordials, spice mixes, marinades and pastes that will become the splashes of colour on the blank canvas of your culinary repertoire.

For me, a dish is more than just a plate of food. It is an idea with which to create a memory. I try to bring diverse elements and emotions into my pictures. We are all suckers for gorgeous photos of food. I want my photography to feed our visual addiction, to tell a story of how the dish came to be and to allow us to dream up delicious moments of our own. I have created beautiful images for these pages and I hope they will not only inspire you to try something new but will also transport you to a lovely imagined world – a bustling street of Morocco, a hip industrial alleyway in downtown Sydney, a rustic farm bench in the country, a trendy café in Germany with the most amazing signage, a chaotic market in India alive with hissing steam, chatter and delicious aromas.

I like to think that with every recipe I cook and with every photograph I capture, I learn something new and share something different with this world. Join me in my wonderful food adventures in *Tasty Express*.

Sneh x

http://www.cookrepublic.com
http://www.facebook.com/cookrepublic
http://www.twitter.com/cookrepublic
http://www.instagram.com/cookrepublic

THINGS TO
REMEMBER

★ All recipes that require baking have been cooked in a conventional oven. You might have to reduce the temperature by 20ºC if you use a fan-forced oven. Regardless, you may have to adjust the temperature depending on your own oven.

★ All recipes have been tested and cooked on an induction cooktop. Cooking times may vary on ceramic or gas cooktops.

★ All eggs used in the recipes are standard eggs (55g).

★ Just about all the ingredients used in the recipes can be easily found in your local supermarkets. You may need to source a few of them – like chaat masala, steel cut oats, wakame, quinoa and Tuscan kale – from specialty grocers, health food stores and delicatessens.

★ I stipulate the use of ginger paste and garlic paste frequently. They are a godsend! You can pick up jars of them at your local supermarket. Of course, you can use fresh ginger and garlic if you like.

CAFE CULTURE

*Breakfast might be quick on some days
and leisurely on others, but it can always be fun!
Bring the hustle and bustle of your favourite cafe into your kitchen
with these recipes. Fresh eggs, naughty granola, healthy breads,
power-packed muffins, pancakes with a twist and wholesome
smoothies all work hard to start your day right!*

Hot Chocolate Chai	4
Mexe Baked Beans	6
House Granola	8
Pick-Me-Up Veggie Muffins	10
Hot Steel-Cut Oats with Cream & Caramelised Fruit	13
Coconut Bircher Muesli with Rose Compote	14
Baked Cinnamon French Toast	16
Masala Omelette Toasties	18
Bacon & Egg Butty with Potato Crisps & Spicy Tomato Chutney	20
Balsamic Mushroom Frittata	25
Roasted Milo & Choc Chip Granola	26
Carrot Cake Muffins	28
Crunchy Top Banana Coconut Bread	30
Big Breakfast Bread	33
Coconut & Jam Sheet Scones	34
Crispy Pancakes with Bombay Potatoes & Fresh Salsa	36
Rum & Raisin Pancakes with Rum Butter Sauce	39

QUICKIES

Grape Lassi
Cocoa Soy Smoothie
Kulfi Milk

40

HOT CHOCOLATE
CHAI

SERVES 4

There is nothing more inviting than slowly simmering a pan of hot chocolate, tea and spices for a morning with friends and letting its warmth and aroma envelope you in a big delicious hug. This chai is best enjoyed with some warm scones (see page 34 for Coconut & Jam Sheet Scones) and good company.

HOT CHOCOLATE

1½ CUPS (375ML) MILK

¼ CUP (60ML) THICKENED CREAM

2½ TABLESPOONS HOT CHOCOLATE POWDER, PLUS EXTRA TO DUST

CHAI

2 TEASPOONS RUSSIAN CARAVAN TEA LEAVES

1 LARGE CINNAMON STICK

2 WHOLE STAR ANISE

To make the chai, combine all the ingredients in a teapot, and add enough boiling water to brew (about 2 cups). Stand for 5 minutes, then strain and set aside. Reserve the cinnamon stick and star anise.

For the hot chocolate, heat the milk and cream in a milk pan on medium heat. When the milk starts foaming at the edges, add the hot chocolate powder and the reserved star anise and cinnamon stick. Add a cup of the strained tea. Simmer, stirring gently and constantly, for about 5 minutes until hot and steamy. Add more of the remaining strained tea if you desire a stronger chai flavour.

Pour in large mugs or glasses, dust with extra chocolate powder and serve immediately.

★ ★ ★

If you don't have Russian Caravan, any strong black tea will do the trick. Tea with chocolate, vanilla or spice notes works best for this recipe. •

I have been cooking a quick batch of homemade herb-baked beans for years. It is part of the symphony of sizzle, crackle, pops and chatter that is our weekend breakfast. Recently, I have been shaking up tradition with this tangy Mexican version. It has a delightful bite that has made it a family favourite. We love it even more with corn chips and sour cream.

MEXE
BAKED BEANS

SERVES 4

2 TABLESPOONS OLIVE OIL

1 RED ONION, FINELY CHOPPED

2 GARLIC CLOVES, MINCED

2 CANS (410G EACH) CANNELLINI BEANS, RINSED AND DRAINED

2 CANS (400G EACH) DICED TOMATOES

1 TABLESPOON CHOPPED THYME LEAVES

1 TABLESPOON GROUND CUMIN

1 TEASPOON DRIED OREGANO

1 TEASPOON SMOKED PAPRIKA

1 TABLESPOON BALSAMIC VINEGAR

1 TABLESPOON TABASCO SAUCE

1 TABLESPOON WORCESTERSHIRE SAUCE

SALT TO TASTE

SOUR CREAM, FRESH AVOCADO AND CORN CHIPS TO SERVE

Heat the oil in a deep, heavy-bottomed saucepan on medium heat. Sauté the onion and garlic until tender. Add the beans, tomato, thyme, cumin, oregano, paprika and balsamic vinegar.

Simmer on medium heat for 15 minutes. Add the Tabasco and Worcestershire sauces. Simmer for another 5 minutes. Season with salt to taste.

Serve topped with a dollop of sour cream, sliced avocado and corn chips.

★ ★ ★

This breakfast dish goes from morning glory to evening stunner in the form of a delicious make-ahead party canapé. I like to serve a platter of corn chips topped with a teaspoon of baked beans, some guacamole and Tabasco sauce.

HOUSE **GRANOLA**

Like a good café, we have a signature granola blend at home. It is a medley of colours and texture and we love its sweet and salty nature. It is gorgeous with the naughty toffee almonds, and just as tempting with cacao nibs instead. It keeps well in my pantry for up to a week. If I am making a small batch, I often stir through an egg white just before baking. This forms those famous granola clusters that everyone loves.

4 CUPS (360G) ROLLED OATS

1 CUP (80G) SHREDDED COCONUT

⅔ CUP (120G) RAISINS

½ CUP (75G) DRIED CRANBERRIES

½ CUP (50G) WALNUTS

¼ CUP (35G) PUMPKIN SEEDS

½ TEASPOON SALT

FINELY GRATED ZEST OF 2 LARGE ORANGES

125G BUTTER

½ CUP (125ML) MAPLE SYRUP

TOFFEE ALMONDS

20G BUTTER

1 TABLESPOON RAW SUGAR

1 TABLESPOON HONEY

½ TEASPOON SALT

1 CUP (180G) ALMONDS

To make the toffee almonds, melt the butter in a heavy-bottomed saucepan on low heat. Add the sugar, honey and salt. Simmer for a few minutes until sugar has dissolved, then add the almonds.

Cook, stirring constantly, for a few minutes until almonds are well coated with the mixture.

Increase the heat slightly and continue cooking for 2–4 minutes till the mixture starts caramelising and becomes sticky. Remove from the heat. Line a baking tray with baking paper and spread the toffee almonds onto the tray. Leave to cool and set.

Preheat the oven to 150°C, and line two baking trays with baking paper. Combine the oats, coconut, toffee almonds, raisins, cranberries, walnuts, pumpkin seeds, salt and zest in a large bowl. Melt the butter and maple syrup on low heat in a heavy-bottomed saucepan, and add to the bowl. Mix well.

Spread the granola mixture evenly across both trays. Bake for about 35 minutes, until golden brown. Turn the trays and swap between top and bottom shelves in the oven half-way through cooking, so the granola browns evenly. Remove from the oven and cool completely.

When cooled, gently scoop clusters of baked granola and store in an airtight container in a cool corner of your pantry for up to two weeks.

These are moreish muffins that fuel you up and take you from breakfast to lunch without a single hunger pang. And they freeze well!

PICK-ME-UP
VEGGIE MUFFINS

MAKES 10

2 CUPS (300G) SELF-RAISING FLOUR

1 TEASPOON SWEET PAPRIKA

¾ TEASPOON SALT

1 LARGE CARROT, GRATED

1 LARGE ZUCCHINI, GRATED

½ CUP SPRING ONIONS, SLICED

¾ CUP (75G) COARSELY GRATED MOZZARELLA
(FOR A LIGHTER TASTE) OR CHEDDAR
(FOR A STRONGER TASTE)

½ CUP (125ML) BUTTERMILK

3 EGGS

60G BUTTER, MELTED

Preheat the oven to 210°C. Spray ten ½ cup capacity muffin pans with oil to grease.

Sift the flour, paprika and salt together into a large bowl. Add the carrot, zucchini, spring onions and cheese. Toss to combine until the flour coats the veggies, and make a well in the centre of the mixture. Whisk the buttermilk, eggs and melted butter in a jug and pour into the well. Using a light hand, gently fold into the muffin mixture with a metal spoon until just combined.

Spoon the mixture into the prepared tins and bake for 20 minutes until golden and springy to a gentle touch. Transfer to a wire rack to cool.

★ ★ ★

To freeze, cool completely. Slice in half and spread with butter, then put the halves back together. Wrap in wax paper and freeze in a zip lock bag.

I love oats for breakfast but I have been disappointed by many a soggy bowl on occasion. When I discovered steel-cut oats, those days were banished forever. Steel-cut oats are the wholegrain inner portion of the oat kernels that have been cut into pieces. They are golden in colour and have a satisfying chewy bite when cooked. I usually make mine express over 20–30 minutes on the stovetop and serve with a dollop of cream and fresh fruit. They are my chilly morning guilty pleasure!

HOT STEEL-CUT OATS
WITH CREAM & CARAMELISED FRUIT

SERVES 1

OATS

¼ TEASPOON SALT

1 CUP (180G) STEEL-CUT OATS

½ TEASPOON GROUND CINNAMON

1 TABLESPOON CREAM

1 TABLESPOON MAPLE SYRUP

CARAMELISED FRUIT

1 TABLESPOON OLIVE OIL

1 SMALL RED APPLE, CORED AND SLICED

1 PEAR, CORED AND SLICED

1 LARGE NECTARINE, HALVED AND PITTED

1 TABLESPOON RAW SUGAR

SQUEEZE OF LEMON JUICE

To cook the oats, combine the salt with 3 cups (750ml) water in a saucepan and bring to the boil on high heat. Add the oats, reduce the heat to low and simmer uncovered for 20–25 minutes. Stir in the cinnamon. Remove from heat.

Meanwhile, for the caramelised fruit, heat a frying pan on high heat, and add the oil. When it is hot, add the fruit to the pan. Sprinkle with the raw sugar and cook for a minute, or until the fruit starts caramelising. Flip once and cook the other side for a few seconds. Remove from the heat and squeeze some lemon juice over. Toss to combine.

Serve the hot oats with the cream, maple syrup and caramelised fruit.

★ ★ ★

Can you believe I only discovered Bircher muesli a few months ago while visiting the beautiful Hunter Valley? The kitchen staff of the hotel where we were staying enthusiastically recommended the chef's special overnight-soaked muesli. The flavours remained with me and so I created this recipe to sate my Bircher muesli cravings.

COCONUT BIRCHER MUESLI
WITH ROSE COMPOTE

SERVES 2

BIRCHER MUESLI MIX

3 CUPS (270G) ROLLED OATS

1 CUP (80G) SHREDDED COCONUT

¼ CUP (25G) WHEATGERM

1 TEASPOON SALT

1 CUP (120G) CRUSHED PECANS

½ CUP (75G) PEPITAS

2 TABLESPOONS MAPLE SYRUP

COCONUT BIRCHER MUESLI

1 CUP (105G) BIRCHER MUESLI MIX

½ CUP (125ML) APPLE JUICE

1¾ CUPS (210G) NATURAL YOGHURT

1 TABLESPOON HONEY

ROSE COMPOTE

2 CUPS (300G) FROZEN MIXED BERRIES

2 TABLESPOONS RAW SUGAR

2 TABLESPOONS ROSE WATER

1 CINNAMON STICK

1 TEASPOON VANILLA EXTRACT

To make the Bircher muesli mix, combine all the ingredients in a large bowl until evenly mixed. This makes 10 serves, but you can store it in an airtight container for up to a week.

For the coconut Bircher muesli, combine all the ingredients in a bowl, and mix well. Cover and refrigerate overnight.

To make the rose compote, combine all the ingredients with 2 tablespoons water in a small saucepan. Bring to a simmer over low heat, and cook for 10 minutes until soft and fragrant. Cool.

To serve, divide the coconut Bircher muesli between serving bowls, and top with the rose compote.

The rose compote keeps well in the fridge for up to a week and can also be used on cakes and puddings.

BAKED CINNAMON
FRENCH TOAST

SERVES 6-8

MELTED BUTTER, TO GREASE

BREADCRUMBS, TO DUST

1 LOAF SOURDOUGH BREAD,
CUT INTO THICK SLICES

1 CUP (250ML) MILK

8 EGGS

½ CUP (125ML) CREAM

2 TABLESPOONS RAW SUGAR

¼ TEASPOON SALT

¼ TEASPOON GROUND CINNAMON,
PLUS EXTRA TO DUST

ICING SUGAR, TO DUST

SHAVED CHOCOLATE, TO SERVE

STRAWBERRIES, TO SERVE

¼ CUP (60ML) MAPLE SYRUP

Preheat the oven to 180°C. Grease a 24cm square baking dish with butter. Dust with breadcrumbs and shake off the excess.

Arrange the bread in the baking dish, making two layers. Combine the milk, eggs, cream, raw sugar, salt and cinnamon in a bowl. Whisk until fluffy and pale. Pour over the bread, making sure it is all covered with egg mixture. Stand for 10 minutes

Place the baking dish into the oven and bake for 30 minutes, until golden and puffed. Remove from the oven and cool slightly.

Dust with the extra cinnamon and icing sugar. Top with shaved chocolate and strawberries. Serve with maple syrup.

★ ★ ★

Growing up, this was my staple after-school snack. I could smell the bread being toasted as I walked through the door with my big blue bag. It is also one of the first things I learned to cook from my mum. A good scrambled egg stuffed in bread and toasted in a jaffle-maker is a fun way to have your morning protein. It also makes a fantastic camping recipe.

MASALA
OMELETTE TOASTIES

MAKES 4

4 EGGS

1 TABLESPOON CREAM

1 TEASPOON GARAM MASALA

SALT & FRESHLY GROUND BLACK PEPPER, TO TASTE

1 TABLESPOON OLIVE OIL

1 RED ONION, FINELY CHOPPED

1 SMALL GREEN CHILLI, FINELY CHOPPED

1/4 CUP (35G) FROZEN PEAS

1/3 CUP FRESH CHOPPED CORIANDER LEAVES

OLIVE OIL SPRAY

8 SLICES WHITE BREAD

KETCHUP (TOMATO SAUCE), TO SERVE

Combine the eggs, cream, garam masala, salt and pepper in a large bowl. Whisk until fluffy.

Heat the oil in a frying pan on high heat. Sauté the onion, chilli, peas and coriander for a few minutes, stirring constantly, until tender. Reduce the heat to low and add the egg mixture. Cook for a few minutes, bringing the egg from the outside of the pan to the centre until just set and wobbly. Remove from the heat.

Heat a jaffle/toastie-maker, and spray with oil. Place one slice of bread on the cooking surface. Top with about 1/4 cup of the egg mixture, and top with another bread slice. Spray the top with more cooking oil and cook the toastie until golden brown. Repeat with the remaining bread and filling.

★ ★ ★

BACON & EGG BUTTY
WITH POTATO CRISPS
& SPICY TOMATO CHUTNEY

SERVES 2, 3 OR 4

1 MEDIUM RED POTATO, THINLY SLICED	**SPICY TOMATO CHUTNEY**
OLIVE OIL SPRAY	1 TABLESPOON OLIVE OIL
2 TABLESPOONS OLIVE OIL	1 TABLESPOON WHOLEGRAIN MUSTARD
1 SMALL BROWN ONION, THICKLY SLICED	1 (400G) CAN DICED TOMATOES
6 RASHERS STREAKY BACON	1 TABLESPOON WORCESTERSHIRE SAUCE
2 EGGS	1 TABLESPOON BROWN SUGAR
1 LARGE CIABATTA LOAF	½ TEASPOON RED CHILLI FLAKES
FEW SPRIGS OF THYME	½ TEASPOON GARAM MASALA
	¼ TEASPOON SALT

To make the spicy tomato chutney, heat the oil in a saucepan on medium heat. Add the mustard and sauté for a few seconds. Add all the other ingredients and reduce heat to low. Simmer, uncovered, for 20 minutes. Transfer to a bowl and cool to room temperature.

Preheat the oven to 220°C and line a baking tray with baking paper. Arrange the potato slices onto the tray in a single layer, and spray lightly with oil. Bake for 15 minutes until starting to become crisp and golden. Remove from the oven and set aside. They will become more crisp as they cool.

Heat the oil in a frying pan on high heat. Add the onion rings and cook for a few minutes on each side, until caramelised and crisp. Remove and set aside. In the same pan, cook the bacon rashers to desired crispness. Remove and set aside.

Wipe out the pan. Heat a tiny bit of oil and fry the eggs until the white has set but the yolk is still soft and runny.

To assemble the butty, cut the ciabatta loaf in half horizontally. Spread the tomato chutney on one side. Top with the onion rings, bacon, potato crisps and eggs. Season with salt and pepper and garnish with thyme sprigs. Place the other piece of the loaf on top to sandwich. Slice into two, three or four individual sandwiches.

★ ★ ★

BALSAMIC MUSHROOM
FRITTATA

SERVES 2

4 EGGS

1 TABLESPOON CREAM

2 TABLESPOONS OLIVE OIL

1 CUP SLICED SWISS BROWN MUSHROOMS

3-4 SPRIGS OF FRESH THYME, LEAVES PICKED

SALT AND FRESHLY GROUND BLACK PEPPER, TO TASTE

¼ CUP (60ML) BALSAMIC VINEGAR

¼ CUP (25G) GRATED CHEDDAR CHEESE

Combine the eggs and cream in a large bowl. Whisk until frothy and pale.

Heat the oil in a frying pan over medium heat. Add the mushrooms and toss until glossy with oil. Add thyme, salt and pepper. Increase the heat to high and add the balsamic vinegar. Cook for a few seconds, until the vinegar evaporates.

Reduce the heat to medium-low. Pour the egg mixture over the mushrooms, and cook for a few minutes until the egg starts to set. Top with the cheese and place under a hot grill until the egg is cooked completely and the cheese is golden.

★ ★ ★

I happened upon this recipe by accident when making a fresh batch of granola while whipping up some malt milk for the kids. I knocked my hand and dropped the Milo in the granola bowl. History was created. True story! This is for the days when you need to satisfy your inner child at breakfast. The delicious combination of chocolate, nuts and oats toasted with your favourite malt drink is a perfect treat. It is also an ideal ice-cream topper. Try it on the Coconut Frozen Yoghurt (page 212)

ROASTED MILO & CHOC CHIP
GRANOLA

MAKES 8 SERVINGS

2 CUPS (180G) ROLLED OATS

1 CUP (35G) RICE BUBBLES

½ CUP (55G) MILO

½ CUP (75G) RAW SHELLED PEANUTS

¼ CUP (60ML) MAPLE SYRUP

40G BUTTER, MELTED

½ TEASPOON SALT

½ CUP (95G) CHOCOLATE CHIPS

Preheat the oven to 180°C. Place all the ingredients except the chocolate chips in a bowl and toss to combine.

Place the mixture onto a baking tray and bake for 15 minutes.

Remove from the oven and cool to just warm. Toss the chocolate chips through the mixture and cool completely. Store in an airtight container for up to a week.

★ ★ ★

CARROT CAKE
MUFFINS

MAKES 12 SMALL OR 6 LARGE

1½ CUPS (225G) PLAIN FLOUR

1 TABLESPOON BROWN SUGAR

2 TEASPOONS BAKING POWDER

2 TEASPOONS GROUND CINNAMON

1 TEASPOON MIXED SPICE

½ TEASPOON SALT

FINELY GRATED RIND OF 1 LEMON

½ CUP CRUSHED PINEAPPLE

1½ CUPS FINELY GRATED CARROT

⅓ CUP (60G) RAISINS

2 EGGS, LIGHTLY BEATEN

½ CUP (125ML) MILK

⅓ CUP (80ML) HONEY

¼ CUP (60ML) VEGETABLE OIL

1 TEASPOON VANILLA EXTRACT

½ CUP (60G) CHOPPED PECANS

1 TABLESPOON ROLLED OATS

RAW SUGAR, TO SPRINKLE

ICING SUGAR, TO DUST

Preheat the oven to 190°C. Grease twelve ½ cup capacity muffin tins (or 6 small latte glasses) and line with parchment paper or paper cups.

Combine the flour in a bowl with the sugar, baking powder, cinnamon, mixed spice and salt. Stir in the lemon rind, pineapple, carrot and raisins. Add the eggs, milk, honey, oil and vanilla extract. Stir through the pecans. Mix gently with a wooden spoon to form a lumpy batter, taking care not to over-mix or the muffins will be tough and rubbery.

Spoon the batter into the prepared paper cases, about two thirds full. Sprinkle rolled oats and raw sugar on top. Bake for about 30 minutes, or until well risen and golden, and springy to a gentle touch.

Cool in the pan before turning out. Serve dusted with icing sugar.

★ ★ ★

CRUNCHY TOP BANANA COCONUT
BREAD

1 CUP (150G) WHITE SPELT FLOUR

1 CUP (90G) DESICCATED COCONUT

¾ CUP (90G) ALMOND MEAL

3 TEASPOONS BAKING POWDER

2 TEASPOONS GROUND CINNAMON

1 TEASPOON NUTMEG

¼ TEASPOON SALT

4 EGGS

¾ CUP (165G) RAW SUGAR

200ML COCONUT MILK

1 CUP MASHED OVERRIPE BANANA

ALMOND FLAKES AND RAW SUGAR TO SPRINKLE

Preheat oven to 190°C. Grease and line a 25cm x 11cm (base measurement) loaf tin with baking paper, overhanging the two long sides.

Combine the spelt flour, coconut, almond meal, baking powder, cinnamon, nutmeg and salt in a bowl. Mix well.

Place the eggs and sugar in a large bowl. Beat with an electric mixer until fluffy and smooth. Add coconut milk and whisk for a minute or two. Add the banana and mix gently with a wooden spoon.

Add the dry mixture to the wet mixture and mix with a wooden spoon until it is well combined. Spoon into the prepared tin. Sprinkle the top with the almond flakes and raw sugar.

Bake for about 45 minutes, until cooked through when tested with a skewer. Cool completely in the tin. Store in an airtight container in the fridge for up to 3 days.

★ ★ ★

You can also bake this with normal plain flour. Dust with cinnamon and icing sugar for a decadent treat.

I have baked many a banana bread over the years. While I have a soft spot for a caramel and chocolate chip version, this healthier take is by far my favourite. It has a beautiful, friand-like texture enhanced by dessicated coconut and almond meal. It is baked without butter or oil but with coconut milk. It smells divine and toasts like a dream!

BIG BREAKFAST BREAD

SERVES 6-8

This is one of the quickest breads you will ever make. It's a spin-off from traditional focaccia, and can be baked with your favourite toppings – ham, sausage, salami, veggies and herbs. Wrap in baking paper, pack in a box and go on a picnic. Perfect for sitting on the lawn and pulling apart with fingers while sharing with friends and family.

1½ TEASPOONS DRY YEAST

2 TEASPOONS CASTER SUGAR

2⅔ CUPS (400G) STRONG WHITE FLOUR

100G FINE SEMOLINA

2 TEASPOONS SALT

2 TABLESPOONS OLIVE OIL

EXTRA FLOUR FOR KNEADING AND DUSTING

10 CHERRY TOMATOES

3 SWISS BROWN MUSHROOMS, SLICED

1 LARGE KRANSKY SAUSAGE, SLICED

3 EGGS

OIL, TO DRIZZLE

FRESH THYME AND OREGANO

SALT FLAKES AND FRESHLY GROUND BLACK PEPPER

¼ CUP (20G) FINELY GRATED PARMESAN CHEESE

Stir the yeast and sugar into 300ml lukewarm water in a small bowl. Set aside for 10 minutes until mixture is frothy and bubbly.

Combine the flour, semolina, salt and olive oil in a large bowl, and make a well in the centre. Pour the yeast mixture into the well. Using a wooden spatula, stir the dough until it comes together loosely.

Dust a work surface with flour. Place the dough onto the flour and knead gently for a few minutes, until dough is smooth. Place the dough ball into a well-oiled bowl and cover with a tea towel. Rest for 30 minutes, until risen. Preheat the oven to 200°C. Line the base and sides of a 20cm square cake pan with baking paper.

Transfer the dough to the prepared pan, stretching to fill all the corners. Make sure the dough is raised around the edges. Arrange the cherry tomatoes, mushrooms and sausages over the dough. Crack the eggs in the gaps. Drizzle with oil and sprinkle with herbs. Bake for 15–20 minutes, until risen and golden brown.

Season with salt and pepper. Serve topped with the parmesan cheese.

Be careful not to overcrowd the bread with toppings. If the egg isn't finished at the end of baking, place under a hot grill until just cooked.

COCONUT & JAM
SHEET SCONES

SERVES 6-8

They say laziness is the mother of invention, don't they? Well, I do! I love scones but dislike cutting out the rounds. So one fine day I baked a sheet scone. It comes baked with jam down the middle. All you have to do is cut up some slices and devour with cream.

3 CUPS (450G) SELF-RAISING FLOUR

1/4 TEASPOON SALT

1 CUP (90G) DESICCATED COCONUT

30G BUTTER, CUBED

1 CUP (250ML) LEMONADE

1 CUP (250ML) THICKENED CREAM

1/2 CUP (165G) BLUEBERRY JAM

MILK, FOR GLAZING

CREAM, TO SERVE

Preheat oven to 180°C. Combine the flour, salt and ¾ cup (70g) of the coconut in a large bowl. Add the butter and rub it with your fingertips until the mixture resembles breadcrumbs. Add the lemonade and cream. Using a wooden spoon, mix gently till the dough just comes together.

Place dough on a generously floured work surface. Knead gently for a minute till it forms a smooth dough. Divide the dough in half. Use a rolling pin to roll out each portion into a rectangular shape about 1.5cm thick.

Place one of the rectangles onto a sheet of baking paper. Spread jam evenly over the dough, and sprinkle the extra coconut evenly on top of the jam. Gently lift the other rectangle and place it over the jam and coconut layer. Press down gently.

Pick up the paper and lift onto a baking tray. Brush the top with milk, to glaze. Bake for 20 minutes, until golden and cooked through.

Using a sharp knife, cut the scones into long thin slices or into squares and serve with cream.

★ ★ ★

You could fill these scones with Nutella or chocolate chips or even passionfruit butter (see page 217). The sky's the limit!

JAM

PANCAKES

1 CUP (150G) CHICKPEA FLOUR (BESAN)

½ CUP (90G) SEMOLINA

¼ CUP (70G) PLAIN YOGHURT

1 TEASPOON SALT

VEGETABLE OIL, FOR FRYING

SWEET CHUTNEY OR HOT RELISH, TO SERVE

SALSA

1 TOMATO, DICED

1 SMALL RED ONION, FINELY CHOPPED

½ CUP FRESH CORIANDER LEAVES

1 TABLESPOON RAW SUGAR

¼ TEASPOON SALT

JUICE OF HALF A LEMON

FOR THE POTATOES

3 POTATOES (600G), PEELED AND DICED

2 TABLESPOONS OLIVE OIL

1 SMALL RED ONION, FINELY CHOPPED

1 TEASPOON MUSTARD SEEDS

1 GREEN CHILLI, SLICED

½ TEASPOON GRATED FRESH GINGER

¼ TEASPOON GROUND TURMERIC

1 TEASPOON GROUND CUMIN

1 TEASPOON RED CHILLI POWDER

SALT, TO TASTE

JUICE OF 1 LEMON

There is a popular street snack in India called masala dosa that is paper-thin crepes stuffed with a spicy potato ragu. I have created an easy express version with these wholesome pancakes and Bombay potatoes. The thinner you spread the batter on the pan, the crispier your pancake will be.

CRISPY PANCAKES
WITH BOMBAY POTATOES & FRESH SALSA

MAKES 8 SERVINGS

To make the pancakes, use a wire whisk to mix all the ingredients with 1¼ cups (310ml) water to a smooth batter. Set aside to rest for 15 minutes.

To make the salsa, mix the ingredients in a bowl. Cover and set aside.

For the potatoes, cook in a saucepan of boiling salted water for 10 minutes, or until just tender. Drain and set aside.

Heat the olive oil in a frying pan on low heat. Add the onion, mustard seeds, chilli and ginger. Sauté for a few minutes until onions are soft. Add the potatoes and mix well. Add the turmeric, cumin, chilli powder and season with salt. Toss to combine. Increase heat to medium, cover and cook for 20 minutes. Remove from heat when potatoes are cooked through, and stir through the lemon juice.

To finish the pancakes, heat a teaspoon of oil in a 24cm (base measurement) crepe pan on high heat. Ladle ½ cup of the pancake batter onto the pan. With a light hand, using the back of the ladle, spread the batter evenly in a large circle. Cook for a few seconds, until bubbles appear on the surface. With a spatula, gently flip the pancake over and cook the other side for a minute. Repeat with the remaining batter.

To serve, top the pancake with potatoes and salsa. Serve with a sweet chutney or hot relish.

★ ★ ★

RUM & RAISIN PANCAKES
WITH RUM BUTTER SAUCE

MAKES 12

PANCAKES

2 CUPS (300G) SELF-RAISING FLOUR

2 EGGS

2 TABLESPOONS CASTER SUGAR

1½ CUPS (375ML) MILK

½ CUP (90G) RAISINS

2 TABLESPOONS RUM

1 TEASPOON VANILLA EXTRACT

PINCH OF SALT

1 TABLESPOON LIGHT OLIVE OIL

RUM BUTTER SAUCE

50G BUTTER

1 TABLESPOON RUM

2 TABLESPOONS RAISINS

⅓ CUP (80ML) MAPLE SYRUP

To make the pancakes, combine all ingredients in a large bowl, and whisk with a wire whisk until smooth. Set aside to rest for 15 minutes.

To make the rum butter sauce, combine all the ingredients in a small heavy-bottomed saucepan on low heat. Simmer until the butter has melted and the raisins are plump. Remove from the heat and leave in the pan to keep warm.

Heat a crepe pan on medium heat. Pour ½ cup pancake batter onto the centre of the hot pan and gently spread the batter to form a circle approximately 14cm in diameter. Cook until bubbles appear on the surface. Using a spatula, gently flip the pancake over and cook the other side for a minute, or until golden. Repeat with the remaining batter.

Serve the pancakes drizzled with the rum butter sauce.

★ ★ ★

QUICKIES

1. GRAPE **LASSI**

SERVES 2

1 CUP (175G) RED SEEDLESS GRAPES

1 TABLESPOON MAPLE SYRUP

½ TEASPOON VANILLA EXTRACT

1 CUP (280G) NATURAL YOGHURT

½ CUP (125ML) MILK

Put all the ingredients in the jug of a blender. Blend until smooth.

★ ★ ★

2. COCOA SOY **SMOOTHIE**

SERVES 2

1 RIPE BANANA

1 RED APPLE, CORED

1 ORANGE, SKIN, PITH AND SEEDS REMOVED

6 ALMONDS

1 TABLESPOON INSTANT OATS

2 TABLESPOONS DARK COCOA POWDER

1 CUP (250ML) SOY MILK

Put all the ingredients in the jug of a blender. Blend until smooth.

★ ★ ★

3. KULFI MILK

½ CUP (65G) UNSALTED PISTACHIO KERNELS
½ CUP (90G) ALMONDS
¼ CUP (55G) CASTER SUGAR
½ TEASPOON GROUND CARDAMOM
¼ TEASPOON SALT
FEW SAFFRON STRANDS

Place the pistachios and almonds in a large heatproof bowl and cover them completely with boiling water. Cover and stand for one hour.

Drain the nuts, and using your fingertips gently peel and rub off the skins. Rinse the nuts and drain well.

Place the nuts in the jug of a blender with 5 cups (1.25 litres) cold water. Process until fine and smooth. Line a big jug or bowl with a nut milk bag or sieve lined with muslin cloth. Pour the nut mixture through the nut milk bag. Press the solids with a wooden spoon to squeeze out the liquid, and leave for about 5 minutes to drain. Discard the nut solids.

Add the sugar, cardamom, salt and saffron to the nut milk. Mix well. Store in a glass bottle in the fridge for up to 3 days.

GREEN KINGDOM

Eating meals loaded with vegetables, seeds and grains
is a real joy if the flavours are fresh and vibrant and the food has
appealing texture and substance. There is never a dull dish in the
green kingdom with spicy croquettes, wholesome salads,
aromatic light soups, bold noodles, vegetarian steaks
and zesty seasonal chutneys.

CHUTNEYS

GARLIC & QUINOA THYME
PATTIES

MAKES ABOUT 20

This has been the most popular recipe on my blog and is one of the easiest and tastiest ways to cook quinoa. Everyone who makes these flavour-packed patties loves them. The marriage of garlic and thyme is a happy one, but when you add chives and paprika to the mix, the party really begins. I cook them for a quick snack; smash them up in a green salad and stick them in the sandwich press with bread and cheese for irresistible hot toasties. They freeze well, so I always have a box cooked and ready in the freezer for a rainy day.

2 ½ CUPS (460G) COOKED QUINOA (SEE PAGE 48)

5 ORGANIC EGGS

½ CUP (40G) FINELY GRATED PARMESAN CHEESE

3 WHOLEMEAL BREAD SLICES, PROCESSED INTO BREADCRUMBS

¼ CUP FINELY CHOPPED CHIVES

3 GARLIC CLOVES, FINELY CHOPPED

1 LARGE RED ONION, FINELY CHOPPED

1 TABLESPOON FINELY CHOPPED FRESH THYME

1 TEASPOON SWEET PAPRIKA

SALT, TO TASTE

VEGETABLE OIL, TO PAN-FRY

KETCHUP

Put all ingredients except the oil and ketchup into a large bowl and mix well with a large wooden spoon until thoroughly combined.

Scoop some mixture in the palm of your hands to shape a patty approximately 5cm in diameter and 1cm thick. This size will yield approximately 20 patties with the mixture you have. (You can make them smaller and thicker, or larger and flatter if you like.)

Heat 1 tablespoon of oil in a large frying pan on medium heat. Gently place 4–5 patties into the pan and shallow-fry, cooking each side for 2 minutes before gently flipping over with a small spatula to cook the other side. Repeat till all the patties are cooked. Use a tablespoon of oil each time you start cooking a new batch of patties.

Serve hot or cold with ketchup (tomato sauce).

These delicate patties are a tad tricky to shape as they may stick to your hands or fall apart in the pan. Gentle handling prevents this. Once they are cooked on one side, they become easier to manage and flatten nicely for even browning. You can make them even easier to work with by adding 1 tablespoon of plain flour.

HOW TO COOK
QUINOA

MAKES APPROXIMATELY 5 CUPS

Quinoa (keen-wah) is the seed of a grain-like crop native to South America. Thanks to its exceptional nutritional qualities and increasing ease of availability, it is becoming popular among adventurous foodies and health-conscious cooks. The quinoa seed has an outer bitter coating that must be rinsed out before cooking. Just like couscous, it is an easy and quick ingredient to make, but, unlike couscous, it must be cooked on the heat. Cooked quinoa has a beautiful nutty flavour and a lovely texture. It freezes well. Frozen quinoa can be thawed overnight in the fridge or for a few hours on your kitchen counter before being used.

2 CUPS (250G) UNCOOKED QUINOA
½ TEASPOON SALT FLAKES
3 CUPS WATER

Place uncooked quinoa into a large bowl and rinse it a couple of times under cold running water. Place the rinsed quinoa, salt and water into a heavy-bottomed saucepan. Bring to a boil on medium heat. Reduce heat to low and simmer uncovered for 15–20 minutes until the water disappears, the quinoa is tender and you can see the little curlicues. Remove from heat. Cool and store in an airtight container in the fridge for up to a week or in the freezer for up to a month.

 ★ ★ ★

Cooked quinoa can be used in porridge and to bake muffins and cakes.

It can be tossed through salads and toasted with nuts and veggies for a healthier alternative to fried rice.

It can be made into burger patties (page 46), sophisticated croquettes (page 56) and used as a stuffing for veggies and meat (page 50).

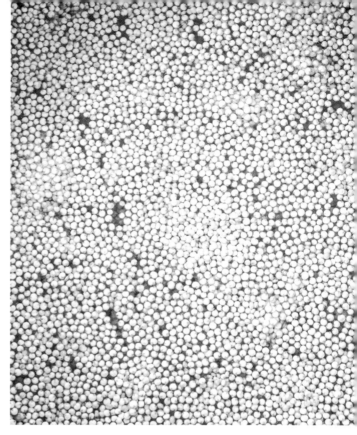

BAKED CAPSICUM
STUFFED WITH QUINOA & NUTS

SERVES 4

4 LARGE RED CAPSICUMS, TOPS SLICED
AND SEEDS REMOVED

3 CUPS (500G) COOKED QUINOA

1½ CUPS (360G) SMOOTH RICOTTA

½ CUP (80G) SULTANAS

½ CUP (50G) FLAKED ALMONDS

1 TABLESPOON CHOPPED FRESH THYME

1½ TEASPOONS SMOKED PAPRIKA

1 TEASPOON SALT

2 TABLESPOONS OLIVE OIL

GRATED PARMESAN, TO SERVE

Preheat the oven to 200°C. Cut the tops from the
capsicum (keep the tops), and scoop out the seeds and
membrane.

Combine the quinoa, ricotta, sultanas, almonds,
thyme, paprika and salt in a large bowl. Mix until well
combined. Scoop this filling into each capsicum and
place the top back on.

Heat oil in a flameproof roasting pan on medium heat.
Add the stuffed capsicums to the pan and cook for a few
minutes until fragrant.

Transfer to the oven, and bake for 30 minutes until the
capsicums have softened and are starting to brown.

Serve hot with grated parmesan.

★ ★ ★

BBQ NOODLE
SALAD

SERVES 6–8

4 PACKETS (70G EACH) DRIED INSTANT NOODLES

2 TABLESPOONS OLIVE OIL

1 SMALL CARROT, JULIENNED

1 SMALL RED CAPSICUM, FINELY SLICED

1 CUP FINELY SLICED CABBAGE

½ CUP PEAS

½ CUP SLICED GREEN BEANS

¼ CUP (60ML) KETCHUP (TOMATO SAUCE)

1 TEASPOON VEGETABLE STOCK POWDER

½ TEASPOON SALT

2 TABLESPOONS WHITE VINEGAR

1 TABLESPOON SOY SAUCE

FRESHLY GROUND BLACK PEPPER, TO TASTE

½ CUP SLICED SPRING ONIONS

¼ CUP CHOPPED CORIANDER LEAVES

Cook the noodles according to packet instructions. Drain, refresh in cold water, then drain again. Set aside.

Heat the oil in a wok on high heat. Sauté the vegetables (except the spring onions) for 2 minutes or until glazed and glossy. Add the noodles and toss to combine.

Add the ketchup, stock powder, salt, vinegar, soy sauce and pepper. Mix well. Cook for 3–5 minutes on high heat.

Serve hot, scattered with the spring onion and coriander.

★ ★ ★

On the streets of Mumbai, especially around a large water body like the curve of a beach or a lake, you'll find colourful, gypsy-like carts selling bhelpuri. This is a popular street snack made from puffed rice, tomatoes, onions, coriander, very fine noodles called sev, chilli, coriander, lemon, black salt and tamarind chutney, among other things. The sweet, sour, tangy and totally addictive dish is the inspiration for this recipe.

CHICKPEA BHEL
SALAD

SERVES 2

400G CAN CHICKPEAS, RINSED AND DRAINED

1 GREEN CAPSICUM, DICED

1 RED ONION, FINELY CHOPPED

1 LEBANESE CUCUMBER, DICED

1 CARROT, GRATED

¼ CUP (35G) ROASTED PEANUTS

LIME WEDGES, TO SERVE

BHEL DRESSING

2 TABLESPOONS OLIVE OIL

1 TABLESPOON GROUND CUMIN

¼ TEASPOON GROUND RED CHILLI

½ TEASPOON CHAAT MASALA

1 TABLESPOON RAW SUGAR

¼ CUP FRESH CORIANDER LEAVES, FINELY CHOPPED

A HANDFUL OF MINT LEAVES

JUICE OF 1 LIME

Combine the chickpeas, capsicum, onion, cucumber, carrot and peanuts in a large bowl and gently toss to coat.

To make the bhel dressing, mix all the ingredients together. Add to the salad and toss to coat. Garnish with lime wedges and serve at a barbecue or on grilled bread with a dollop of tomato chutney.

★ ★ ★

Chaat masala can be found in Indian grocery stores or online specialty grocers. For a more tangy flavour it can be replaced by black salt, also available from these places.

If you have ever eaten at an Indian restaurant or ordered take-away, you could not have missed the samosa, a pyramid-shaped, deep-fried pastry stuffed with a delicious vegetarian filling. These croquettes offer a healthier version. What I love about them is their versatility. They can be shaped like burger patties to provide an excellent vegetarian option for your friends at a barbecue. They can be stuffed inside wraps or pita breads with lashings of spicy sauce and green salad for a nutritious meal. They are perfect lunchbox fillers and, dressed up right, make a sophisticated canapé at your next party.

QUINOA SPICE
CROQUETTES

MAKES 12–15

1 TABLESPOON OLIVE OIL, PLUS EXTRA TO PAN-FRY

2 GARLIC CLOVES, FINELY CHOPPED

½ CUP FRESH OR FROZEN PEAS

2 LARGE POTATOES, BOILED, PEELED AND MASHED

1 CUP (185G) COOKED QUINOA (SEE PAGE 48)

¼ CUP CHOPPED FRESH CORIANDER LEAVES

2 TEASPOONS GROUND CUMIN

1 TEASPOON GARAM MASALA

SALT, TO TASTE

SALAD LEAVES AND SRIRACHA SAUCE, TO SERVE

Heat 1 tablespoon oil in a frying pan on medium heat. Add the garlic and peas. Sauté for a minute or until soft. Remove from the heat and tip into a large bowl. Wipe the pan clean and set aside.

Add the potatoes, quinoa, coriander, cumin and garam masala to the garlic and peas. Season with salt. Mix well and form into slightly flattened oblong croquettes.

Heat 1 tablespoon of oil in the frying pan on medium-high heat. When the oil is hot, add 4–5 croquettes to the pan (depending on the size of the pan). Cook each side for about 4 minutes, flipping gently till golden on both sides.

Repeat with remaining croquettes and oil. Serve hot with salad leaves and sriracha sauce.

★ ★ ★

Sriracha sauce is a Thai chilli sauce. It is available from most large supermarkets in the Asian section.

KALE
TABBOULI

*The traditional parsley-driven tabbouli
with its strong peppery taste gets a modern
makeover with kale as the star ingredient.
This is a fresh, nutrient-rich salad full of
crunch and crisp, clean flavours.*

1 CUP (180G) BULGHUR

1 CUP FINELY CHOPPED TUSCAN KALE

1 CUP FINELY DICED CUCUMBER

¼ CUP FINELY CHOPPED PARSLEY

¾ CUP FINELY SLICED SPRING ONIONS

10 CHERRY TOMATOES, HALVED

½ CUP POMEGRANATE SEEDS

½ CUP CHOPPED MINT LEAVES

2 TABLESPOONS OLIVE OIL

JUICE OF 1 LEMON

1 TEASPOON SALT

FRESHLY GROUND BLACK PEPPER, TO TASTE

Place the bulghur into a bowl and add 1¼ cups
(310ml) hot water. Stand for 10 minutes or
until the bulghur has absorbed the water.
Fluff up the grains with a fork.

Add all the other ingredients and mix well.

★ ★ ★

MUST DO THIS WEEKEND:

PICK SOME FRUIT

GATHER SOME EGGS

CHASE SOME CHOOKS

FEED THE BIRDS

SPY ON THE KANGAROOS

GET HANDS DIRTY

BROWN RICE BIRYANI
SALAD

1 ¼ TEASPOON SALT

1 ¼ CUPS (265G) BROWN RICE

¼ CUP (60ML) OLIVE OIL

1 BAY LEAF

⅓ CUP (50G) CASHEWS

⅓ CUP (55G) SULTANAS

1 LARGE ONION, THINLY SLICED

1 SMALL CARROT, JULIENNED

½ CUP SLICED BEANS

½ CUP SLICED PURPLE CABBAGE

JUICE OF ½ LEMON

2 TEASPOONS GARAM MASALA

½ TEASPOON GROUND CINNAMON

½ TEASPOON GROUND CARDAMOM

SALT, TO TASTE

½ CUP FRESH CORIANDER LEAVES TO SERVE

Combine 2 cups water and the salt in a saucepan on high heat, and bring to the boil. Add the rice when water is boiling. Cook for a minute, then reduce heat to low and cover with a lid.

Simmer for 20 minutes, or until the rice has absorbed all the water. Remove from heat and allow to rest with the lid on for 5 minutes. Fluff with a fork.

Heat the oil in a large sauté pan on medium heat. Add the bay leaf, cashews and sultanas. Stir-fry for a minute, until the nuts start turning golden and the sultanas are plump. Add the onion, carrot and beans. Sauté for 2 minutes until the vegetables are glossy.

Add the cabbage, lemon juice, garam masala, cinnamon, cardamom and salt. Increase heat to high and sauté for a minute until everything is well combined. Remove from heat.

Add the rice to the pan and toss to mix well. Top with coriander leaves, and serve warm.

★ ★ ★

This super healthy, iron-rich soup is a breeze to make. The grilled paneer croutons not only look pretty, they also add delightful contrast and texture.

SPINACH & KALE SOUP
WITH GRILLED CHEESE

SERVES 4

20G BUTTER

1 BAY LEAF

½ CUP CHOPPED BROWN ONION

2 CUPS CHOPPED ENGLISH SPINACH LEAVES

1 CUP CHOPPED KALE LEAVES

1 LARGE POTATO, BOILED, PEELED AND CHOPPED

600ML VEGETABLE STOCK

SALT AND FRESHLY GROUND BLACK PEPPER, TO TASTE

100G PANEER

Melt the butter in a saucepan on medium heat. Add the bay leaf and onion. Sauté until the onion is soft. Add the spinach, kale and potato. Sauté for a minute or two. Add the stock. Cover and simmer for 20 minutes.

Remove the bay leaf from the soup. Purée the soup using a hand blender until smooth. Return to heat and season if desired.

Cut the cheese into cubes or triangle shapes. Place on a dry frying pan and cook each side until golden.

Spoon the soup into bowls, and serve with the grilled cheese.

★ ★ ★

Paneer is an Indian-style cheese. Make sure you buy slab paneer that can be cut into pieces from the cheese aisle at the supermarkets or the frozen section in an Indian grocery store. It can be substituted with halloumi.

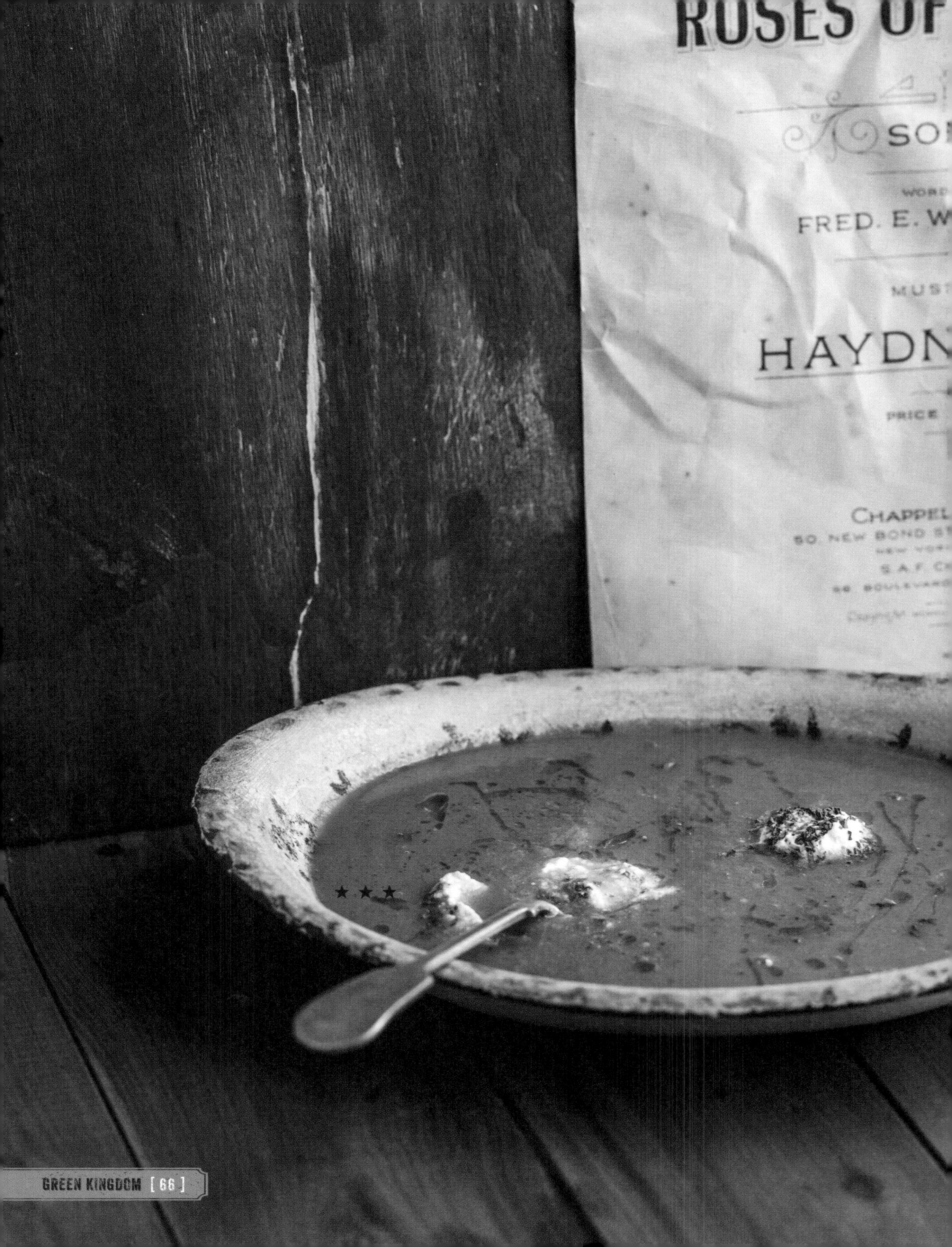
ROSES OF
FRED. E. W
HAYDN
PRICE
CHAPPEL
50, NEW BOND ST

I like to make this soup with the season's biggest and juiciest red tomatoes. It has such a beautiful umami flavour, complemented by the soft tang of the basil labne. Labne cheese is easy to make by draining yoghurt. You can also drop the rolled labne balls into a jar of good-quality olive oil to be used on a cheese platter later.

ROAST TOMATO SOUP
WITH BASIL LABNE

SERVES 4

LABNE

1 CUP GREEK YOGHURT

ABOUT ¼ CUP DRIED BASIL

SOUP

8 MEDIUM TOMATOES, HALVED

OLIVE OIL SPRAY

SALT AND FRESHLY GROUND BLACK PEPPER, TO TASTE

1 TABLESPOON OLIVE OIL

1 BAY LEAF

1 CUP (250ML) VEGETABLE STOCK

1 TEASPOON BALSAMIC VINEGAR

1 TEASPOON SWEET PAPRIKA

1 TEASPOON SUGAR

SALT, TO TASTE

To make the labne, place a sieve over a bowl, making sure there is plenty of clearance between the sieve and the bottom of the bowl. Line the sieve with two layers of cheesecloth. Spoon the yoghurt onto the cheesecloth. Gather up the ends of the cheesecloth and twist to enclose. Place a heavy weight (like a couple of cans on a saucer) on top of the parcel and place in the fridge for an hour to drain.

Unwrap the drained yoghurt. Using a spoon, roll balls of yoghurt about the size of a golf ball. Roll the balls gently in dried basil. Set aside in the fridge until needed.

To make the soup, preheat the oven to 190°C and line a baking tray with baking paper. Place the tomatoes cut side up onto the tray. Spray with oil and season with salt and pepper. Roast for 30 minutes. Cool slightly, then purée.

Heat the oil in a saucepan. Add the bay leaf, pureed tomatoes, stock, balsamic vinegar, paprika, sugar and salt. Bring to the boil, reduce the heat to low and simmer for 20 minutes.

To serve, ladle the soup into bowls, and gently float the labne balls in the hot soup.

★ ★ ★

PUMPKIN & FETA TARTINES

SERVES 4

2 CUPS CUBED PUMPKIN

2 GARLIC CLOVES, UNPEELED

OLIVE OIL SPRAY

8 THICK SLICES SOURDOUGH BREAD

OIL, FOR BRUSHING

1 CUP (200G) CRUMBLED FETA CHEESE

½ CUP (120G) SMOOTH RICOTTA CHEESE

SALT AND FRESHLY GROUND BLACK PEPPER, TO TASTE

HANDFUL OF PINE NUTS

SNOW PEA SPROUTS, TO SERVE

BALSAMIC VINEGAR AND OLIVE OIL, TO DRIZZLE

Preheat the oven to 220°C, and line a baking tray with baking paper. Arrange the pumpkin and garlic on the tray, spray with oil and bake for 30 minutes until tender and starting to brown. Cool.

Brush the bread slices with oil and toast on a chargrill pan on both sides until the edges are slightly charred. Mix the roasted garlic (squeezed out of the skin), feta cheese, ricotta cheese, salt and pepper in a bowl.

Spread the toasted bread slices with cheese mixture. Top with the roasted pumpkin, pine nuts and snow pea sprouts. Drizzle with balsamic vinegar and olive oil.

★ ★ ★

A short drive away through the meandering Galston Gorge near my home lies the wonderful farming community of Dural. At the weekends, we pack a picnic and head to Fagan Park, which has more than seven themed gardens, a lake and rolling grassy hills for sitting on and soaking up the sun. Dotted on either side of the road there are farm gates with 'honesty' boxes. You pick the unattended goods you desire and drop money in the box. Occasionally a farmer will be arranging the freshly picked produce and welcome you like a long-lost friend. Those are treasured moments – like the time I bought a 3kg bag of the freshest broccoli I had ever seen from a dear old lady. She let me in on a secret, which was to cook the broccoli stalks because they are the best part of the vegetable. This delectable dish is a result of that little meeting. It is almost like a pickle that you can layer in your sandwiches.

BUTTERED
BROCCOLI STALKS

SERVES 2

40G BUTTER

1 TABLESPOON WHOLEGRAIN MUSTARD

2 TABLESPOONS HONEY

2 CUPS SLICED BROCCOLI STALKS (FROM 3 HEADS)

¼ CUP (60ML) VEGETABLE STOCK

¼ CUP (25G) FLAKED ALMONDS

FRESH HERBS OR SPROUTS, TO SERVE

Melt the butter in a frying pan on high heat. Add the mustard and honey, then the broccoli stalks. Sauté for a few seconds until the stalks are glazed. Add the vegetable stock, and cook until the stock evaporates.

Remove from the heat and stir through the almonds. Serve warm, with fresh herbs or sprouts.

★ ★ ★

Sushi is my favourite food. I could eat it every single day of my life. And I am always experimenting with interesting ways to prepare it. This deconstructed sushi bowl has all the individual elements and flavours of sushi without the tedious rolling. The best thing is that you can mix it up whenever you make it by adding salmon, chicken, prawn, avocado or even mushrooms.

CITRUS
SUSHI BOWL

SERVES 4

3 CUPS (660G) SUSHI RICE

1 CUP FROZEN EDAMAME BEANS

4 STRIPS OF DRIED WAKAME

1 SMALL EGGPLANT, SLICED

½ CUP POMEGRANATE SEEDS

1 BUNCH CHIVES, CHOPPED

½ CUP CORIANDER LEAVES, CHOPPED

1 SHEET NORI, CUT INTO STRIPS

JAPANESE CITRUS DRESSING

JUICE AND FINELY GRATED ZEST OF 1 LEMON

JUICE AND FINELY GRATED ZEST OF 1 ORANGE

2 TABLESPOONS MIRIN

3 TABLESPOONS RICE VINEGAR

2 TABLESPOONS TAMARI SAUCE

1 TABLESPOON PONZU SAUCE

1 TABLESPOON HONEY

1 TABLESPOONS SESAME SEEDS

To make the Japanese citrus dressing, combine all the ingredients in a bowl.

Place the rice into a sieve and rinse under cold running water. Drain well. Place washed rice with 3 cups (750ml) water in a large saucepan, and bring to boil. Reduce the heat to low, cover and simmer for about 10 minutes, or until the water is absorbed. Remove from heat and stand, covered, for 10 minutes until slightly cooled. Drizzle with the Japanese citrus dressing and mix thoroughly, breaking up the lumps in the rice with a wooden spoon.

Place the edamame beans into a heatproof bowl and cover with boiling water. Stand for 1 minutes, then drain and plunge into a bowl of iced water. Drain and set aside.

Soak the wakame in a bowl of cold water for 10–20 minutes, until tender and increased to about 3 times its original size. Drain and set aside.

Heat a chargrill pan, and cook the eggplant slices for 3–4 minutes each side, until tender and slightly charred.

To prepare the sushi bowl, divide the rice among four bowls. Arrange the edamame beans, eggplant, pomegranate and wakame on the rice. Top with chives, coriander and nori.

Frozen edamame beans, wakame and ponzu sauce are available from Asian grocery stores and some health food stores.

★ ★ ★

Kachumber is a fresh chopped salad from India enlivened by the appearance of sour and tangy green mango. It is incredibly refreshing and tastes even better when chilled.

KACHUMBER
PAPPADUMS

SERVES 8

20 COOKED MINI PAPPADUMS

KACHUMBER SALAD

1 RED ONION, FINELY DICED

1 LARGE LEBANESE CUCUMBER, FINELY DICED

2 LARGE TOMATOES, FINELY DICED

¼ CUP FINELY DICED GREEN MANGO

½ CABBAGE, FINELY SHREDDED THEN CHOPPED

½ CUP FINELY CHOPPED FRESH CORIANDER LEAVES

JUICE OF ½ LEMON

½ TEASPOON SALT

1–2 TABLESPOONS RAW SUGAR

FRESHLY GROUND BLACK PEPPER, TO TASTE

¼ CUP FINELY CHOPPED MINT LEAVES

Put all the ingredients for the salad into a large bowl and toss until well combined.

Serve the salad with pappadums for scooping.

This is such a popular canapé at my get-togethers. Even the kids love it! It looks like heaps of fun and comes together in just under 10 minutes.

DUKKAH CRUSTED BOCCONCINI
LOLLIPOPS

SERVES 8

20–30 BABY BOCCONCINI CHEESE

EXTRA VIRGIN OLIVE OIL, TO SERVE

DUKKAH

½ CUP (65G) UNSALTED PISTACHIO KERNELS

2 TABLESPOONS CORIANDER SEEDS

2 TABLESPOONS SESAME SEEDS

1 TABLESPOON GROUND CUMIN

¼ TEASPOON SALT

¼ TEASPOON RED CHILLI FLAKES

For the dukkah, place all ingredients into a dry frying pan. Toast the mix on low heat for 5–8 minutes until fragrant, stirring often. Remove from the heat and grind coarsely using a mortar and pestle.

Skewer the bocconcini cheese with lollipop sticks and serve on a platter with dukkah and olive oil for dipping.

★ ★ ★

ZUCCHINI NOODLES
WITH THAI PESTO

SERVES 4

This is one of my special recipes that I make time and time again. It is like a cold, green version of Pad Thai with all the sweet, sour, salty and spicy flavours enhanced by the crunch of the peanuts. It is also one of the best ways to eat raw zucchini, shredded into long, noodle-like ribbons with a julienne peeler. A great make-ahead lunch or picnic dish.

100G RICE VERMICELLI NOODLES,
COOKED AND DRAINED

2 LARGE ZUCCHINI, JULIENNED

½ CUP (80G) CRUSHED PEANUTS

LIME WEDGES, TO SERVE

THAI PESTO

¼ CUP (40G) RAW PEANUTS

½ CUP CORIANDER LEAVES

½ CUP BASIL LEAVES

1 TEASPOON RED CHILLI FLAKES

JUICE AND FINELY GRATED ZEST OF 1 LIME

1 GARLIC CLOVE

2.5CM PIECE OF GINGER

2 TEASPOONS FISH SAUCE

1½ TABLESPOONS BROWN SUGAR

½ TEASPOON SALT

⅓ CUP (80ML) OLIVE OIL

For the Thai pesto, place all the ingredients into the bowl of a food processor, and process to a coarse pesto consistency. Set aside.

Place the cooled rice noodles into a large bowl and top with the zucchini. Add the pesto and toss to mix well. Top with crushed peanuts and serve with lime wedges.

★ ★ ★

Julienne peelers are available in most kitchenware stores and look like a vegetable peeler with little sharp teeth around the blade.

EGGPLANT LASAGNE STEAKS

SERVES 6

Eggplants are a boon to vegetarians. They boast a meaty, robust flavour, yet have the honour of belonging to the plant kingdom. In this recipe, I have drawn from traditional Italian tastes and created eggplant lasagne steaks topped with homemade pesto, mushroom, tomato and cheese, and then roasted to perfection.

LARGE EGGPLANT, CUT INTO 6 THICK ROUND SLICES

SMALL VINE-RIPENED TOMATOES

CUP SLICED SWISS BROWN MUSHROOMS

2 BABY BOCCONCINI CHEESE

HANDFUL OF PINE NUTS

PARMESAN CHEESE, TO TASTE

OIL FOR DRIZZLING

PESTO

1 CUP BASIL LEAVES

¼ CUP (20G) FINELY GRATED PARMESAN CHEESE

2 SMALL GARLIC CLOVES

¼ CUP (40G) PINE NUTS

¼ CUP (60ML) OLIVE OIL

To make the pesto, place all the ingredients into the bowl of a food processor, and process to a coarse paste. Season with salt and freshly ground black pepper to taste. Set aside.

Preheat the oven to 190°C. Heat a chargrill pan on medium heat. Place the eggplant slices on the pan and cook for a few minutes on either side until they get the charred line pattern.

Place the eggplant slices on a baking tray, and spread pesto liberally over each slice. Place a whole tomato and two slices of mushroom onto each eggplant slice. Add two bocconcini cheeses per slice. Sprinkle with pine nuts and grate parmesan generously over the top.

Drizzle with olive oil and bake for 30 minutes, until the eggplant is cooked. Season with salt and pepper.

★ ★ ★

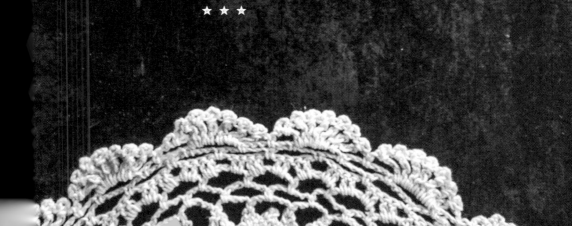

CHUTNEYS

1. BEETROOT & RHUBARB CHUTNEY

MAKES 1.5 CUPS

2 TABLESPOONS OLIVE OIL

½ CUP FINELY CHOPPED ONION

1 CUP PEELED AND COARSELY CHOPPED BEETROOT

1 CUP CHOPPED GREEN APPLE

½ CUP CHOPPED RHUBARB

1 TABLESPOON BALSAMIC VINEGAR

1 TABLESPOON MALT VINEGAR

2 TABLESPOONS RAW SUGAR

½ TEASPOON DRIED THYME LEAVES

Heat the oil in a heavy-bottomed saucepan on medium heat. Add the onion and beetroot. Sauté for a few minutes until onions are tender.

Add the apple, rhubarb, balsamic vinegar, malt vinegar, sugar, thyme and ½ cup (125ml) water. Reduce the heat to low and simmer with the lid on for about 30 minutes, until soft.

Store in a clean, dry glass jar in the fridge for up to a week.

★ ★ ★

2. LUSTY CHUTNEY

MAKES 1.5 CUPS

1 CUP DESEEDED AND FINELY CHOPPED RED CAPSICUM

2 TABLESPOONS VEGETABLE OIL

1 CUP FINELY CHOPPED RED ONION

3 GARLIC CLOVES, MINCED

1 CUP FINELY DICED TOMATO

½ TEASPOON RED CHILLI FLAKES

1 TEASPOON MUSTARD POWDER

2 TABLESPOONS WORCESTERSHIRE SAUCE

2 TABLESPOONS BROWN SUGAR

1 TABLESPOON RED WINE VINEGAR

¼ TEASPOON SMOKED PAPRIKA

1½ TEASPOONS SALT

Preheat the oven to 200°C and line a baking tray with baking paper. Spread the capsicum on the tray. Roast for 10–12 minutes, until some pieces start charring around the edges. Remove from the oven and set aside.

Heat the oil in a heavy-bottomed saucepan on medium heat. Add the onion and garlic, and cook until tender. Add the tomatoes and capsicum, and sauté for two minutes.

Stir in the chilli flakes, mustard powder, Worcestershire sauce, brown sugar, red wine vinegar, paprika and salt. Cook for a minute or two.

Reduce the heat to low and add 1 cup (250ml) water. Simmer uncovered for 45 minutes, until the chutney thickens and comes together. Cool completely.

Store in a clean, dry glass jar in the fridge for up to a week.

★ ★ ★

3. SUPER GREEN CHUTNEY

MAKES 2 CUPS

1 CUP CORIANDER LEAVES AND CHOPPED STALKS

1 CUP BABY SPINACH LEAVES

2 LARGE TUSCAN KALE LEAVES, STALK TRIMMED

1 TABLESPOON CHOPPED GINGER

1 GARLIC CLOVE

¼ CUP (40G) PINE NUTS

¼ CUP MINT LEAVES

JUICE OF ½ LEMON

1 TEASPOON SALT

1 SMALL GREEN CHILLI

1 TABLESPOON SUGAR

1 TABLESPOON PEPITAS

10 CURRY LEAVES

Place all ingredients in the bowl of a food processor with ¼ cup (60ml) water, and blend until smooth.

Store in a clean, dry glass jar in the fridge for up to a week.

★ ★ ★

URBAN LUNCHBOX

A delicious and nourishing lunch takes you through
the afternoon without wanting to dip into the cookie jar. This chapter
lets you create the vibe of the food van or hip urban cafe at home or
in your lunchbox. Add crunchy salads, healthy breads, make-ahead
tarts, veggie burgers, smoky flatbreads, power-packed couscous
and sprouts to your everyday menu.

MUNCHIES

Thai-spiced Lime Almonds
Baked Spinach Crispies
Wholemeal Rosemary Cookies

LUNCHBOX
COUSCOUS

This is my go-to lunchbox staple. I love the explosion of bright flavours in every mouthful and it is equally appealing warm or cold. It goes from wholesome workday lunch fare to a fancy dinner side dish in minutes. It can also be easily customised with whatever you have on hand.

1 TABLESPOON BUTTER

2 TEASPOONS SALT

1 TEASPOON SWEET PAPRIKA

1 TEASPOON DRIED THYME

1 TEASPOON DRIED ROSEMARY

1 TEASPOON GARLIC GRANULES

2 CUPS (400G) COUSCOUS

2 TABLESPOONS WHITE VINEGAR

JUICE OF HALF A LIME

A DASH OF OLIVE OIL

1 CUP CUBED ROASTED PUMPKIN

1 CUP (60G) SUNDRIED TOMATOES, CHOPPED

½ CUP (180G) WHOLE KALAMATA OLIVES

100G GOAT'S MILK FETA CHEESE, CUBED

2 CUPS CHOPPED SPINACH LEAVES

½ CUP CHOPPED SPRING ONIONS

Place the butter, salt, paprika, thyme, rosemary and garlic granules into a large saucepan with 2 cups (500ml) water. Bring to the boil, then remove from the heat. Add the couscous and vinegar and set aside uncovered for 30 minutes until the couscous has absorbed the water and has completely cooled. Fluff up the couscous gently with a fork.

Add the lime juice, olive oil, pumpkin, sundried tomatoes, olives, feta cheese, spinach and spring onions. Toss gently until evenly combined.

Pack in lunch containers and store in the fridge for up to 3 days.

★ ★ ★

GREEN WITH ENVY
FRITTATA

SERVES 8

This frittata is like an edible canvas that you can paint on with seasonal ingredients. I have fun exploring the markets for new green ingredients to put in my frittata whenever I make it.

2 TEASPOONS BUTTER

1 TABLESPOON OLIVE OIL

8 ZUCCHINI FLOWERS

1 CUP BROCCOLI FLORETS

12 ASPARAGUS SPEARS, WOODY BITS TRIMMED

¼ CUP (60ML) WHITE WINE

8 EGGS

½ CUP CHOPPED SPRING ONIONS

⅓ CUP (80G) SOUR CREAM

¼ CUP (20G) SHREDDED PARMESAN CHEESE, PLUS EXTRA FOR SERVING

½ TEASPOON SALT

Heat the butter and oil in a large frying pan on high heat. Add the zucchini flowers, broccoli and asparagus. Sauté for a few seconds. Add the white wine and cook for a minute or two until the wine evaporates. Remove from the heat and set aside.

Preheat the oven to 200°C, and grease a 30cm x 20cm x 4cm ovenproof dish with oil. Place the eggs into a large bowl with the spring onions, sour cream, parmesan cheese and salt. Season with freshly ground black pepper. Whisk with a wire whisk until the eggs are foamy and everything is well combined. Add the vegetables and mix once gently.

Carefully pour the egg and vegetable mixture into the prepared dish. Bake for about 12 minutes or until set. You may pop the dish under a hot grill for a few minutes to brown the top. Remove from the oven, cool and cut into slices. Garnish with the extra parmesan.

★ ★ ★

BISTRO
SALAD

SERVES 4

*I love the contrasting flavours in this bold, vivacious bowl of salad.
The crunch from the nuts and the tart juices of the blood orange go
so well with the goat's cheese. It is a re-creation of a beautiful salad
I always order at my favourite local café.*

6 BABY BEETROOT	1 TABLESPOON BALSAMIC VINEGAR
SPRAY OF COOKING OIL	1 CUP WATERCRESS SPRIGS
3 PEARS, TRIMMED AND QUARTERED	1 CUP ROCKET
1 TABLESPOON HONEY	1 CUP BABY SPINACH
1 TABLESPOON LEMON JUICE	1 CUP (100G) TOASTED WALNUTS
1 TABLESPOON OLIVE OIL	150G GOAT'S CHEESE, CRUMBLED
2 TABLESPOONS FRESH BLOOD ORANGE JUICE	

Preheat the oven to 200°C. Wash the beetroot well and trim the
stems. Pat dry. Place onto a baking tray and spray with oil. Roast
for 45–50 minutes, or until tender when pierced with a small sharp
knife. Set aside until cool enough to handle. Using a sharp vegetable
knife, gently peel off the skin and tops. This will happen quite easily.
Cut into quarters.

Meanwhile, heat a frying pan on medium heat. Add the pears, honey
and lemon juice. Toss to combine and cook for a few seconds until
the pears start caramelising. Remove from the heat and cool.

Combine the olive oil, blood orange juice and balsamic vinegar in
a small bottle with a tight-fitting lid. Shake until well mixed.

Place the beetroot, watercress, rocket, walnuts, goat's cheese and
pears in a large bowl. When ready to serve, add the blood orange
dressing and toss to mix well. Season with salt and freshly ground
black pepper.

If blood oranges are out of
season, use Valencia or navel
– whichever is in season.

My mum had a little round portable oven that she mostly used for baking her best butter cakes from homemade butter. Sometimes she would bake a savoury cake full of spices, nuts and seeds. It tasted fantastic and I was intrigued by the idea of a cake that wasn't sweet. This bread is a take on that memorable recipe. It makes a dense loaf of bread that is gluten-free and nutritious. The long resting time is vital to the distinctive sour flavour, but so worth it! I love it toasted with some sweet chutney.

SOUR CHICKPEA
BREAD
SERVES 8

½ CUP (75G) CHICKPEA FLOUR (BESAN)

½ CUP (90G) RICE FLOUR

1 CUP (170G) CORNMEAL

1½ CUPS (420G) YOGHURT

1½ TEASPOONS SALT

¼ TEASPOON TURMERIC

½ CUP SHREDDED ZUCCHINI (SEE NOTE)

½ CUP SHREDDED CARROT

1½ TABLESPOONS FINELY GRATED GINGER

2 GARLIC CLOVES, MINCED

2 TEASPOONS DRIED RED CHILLI FLAKES

JUICE OF 1 LEMON

1 TEASPOON BAKING POWDER

½ TEASPOON BICARBONATE OF SODA

SUPER GREEN CHUTNEY, TO SERVE
(SEE PAGE 85)

TOPPING

2 TABLESPOONS VEGETABLE OIL

1 TEASPOON MUSTARD SEEDS

1 TEASPOON SESAME SEEDS

¼ CUP WHOLE HAZELNUTS

2 TABLESPOONS PEPITAS

1 TABLESPOON SHREDDED COCONUT

1-2 TABLESPOONS RAW SUGAR

Combine the chickpea flour, rice flour, cornmeal, yoghurt, salt and turmeric in a large bowl. Add 1 cup (250ml) hot water and mix until smooth. Cover with a tea towel and rest in a warm spot for 2 hours, until the mixture looks lighter with bubbles and smells sour.

Add the zucchini, carrot, ginger, garlic, chilli flakes, lemon juice, baking powder and bicarbonate of soda to the flour mixture. Whisk with a balloon whisk until the mixture feels light and airy. Cover and rest in a warm spot for 20 minutes.

Preheat the oven to 200°C. Grease a 23cm x 15cm (base measurement) loaf tin and line with baking paper, hanging over the two long sides. Gently spoon the bread batter into the prepared tin. Take care not to mix or handle the mixture too much at this stage in order to retain the airiness of the batter.

To make the topping, heat the oil in a small frying pan on high heat. Add the mustard and sesame seeds. When they start crackling, add the hazelnuts, pepitas, coconut and sugar. Mix once and remove from heat immediately. Pour evenly over the bread batter. Bake for 40–50 minutes or until risen, golden and a skewer inserted into the middle comes out clean.

Turn off the heat and leave in the oven to cool completely. Serve with Super Green Chutney.

Squeeze handfuls of zucchini over the sink to remove excess liquid. You could bake this in a 20cm round cake tin if you like.

FRIED CHICKEN
WITH HOT GARLIC SAUCE

SERVES 4

*We usually don't fry things at home, preferring to grill or bake instead.
But once in a while I make an exception for this fried chicken dish. It
is sensational and surprisingly light!*

500G CHICKEN THIGH FILLETS, CUT INTO THIN STRIPS	**SAUCE**
1 TABLESPOON GINGER PASTE	2 TABLESPOONS OLIVE OIL
1 TABLESPOON SOY SAUCE	2 TABLESPOONS FINELY CHOPPED GARLIC
2 TABLESPOONS CORNFLOUR	2 TABLESPOONS FINELY CHOPPED RED ONION
1 EGG, LIGHTLY BEATEN	1 TABLESPOON FINELY CHOPPED CORIANDER STALKS
VEGETABLE OIL, FOR DEEP-FRYING	1 SMALL GREEN OR RED CHILLI, FINELY SLICED
1 CUP FINELY SLICED SNOW PEAS	1 TABLESPOON SOY SAUCE
½ CUP FINELY SLICED CABBAGE	1 TABLESPOON WHITE VINEGAR
½ CUP JULIENNED CARROTS	1 TABLESPOON CHILLI SAUCE
½ CUP CHOPPED SPRING ONIONS	1 TABLESPOON TOMATO SAUCE
	½ CUP (125ML) CHICKEN STOCK
	1 TEASPOON CORNFLOUR
	A DASH OF WHITE PEPPER

Mix the chicken, ginger, soy sauce, cornflour and egg in a bowl.
Season with salt. Set aside for 10 minutes. Half-fill a medium
saucepan with oil, and heat on medium heat. Deep-fry the chicken
in batches until golden. Drain on paper towels and place into a large
salad bowl. Add the vegetables to the bowl, over the chicken.

To make the sauce, heat the oil in a small saucepan on medium heat.
Add the garlic, onion, coriander stalks and chilli. Sauté, stirring
constantly, for a few seconds or until starting to brown. Add the soy
sauce, vinegar, chilli sauce, tomato sauce and chicken stock. Reduce
the heat to low and simmer for 2 minutes. Mix the cornflour with
2 tablespoons of water, and add to the pan. Simmer for 5 minutes
or until the sauce thickens. Season with salt and white pepper. Pour
the hot sauce over the chicken and vegetables, and toss to combine.

★ ★ ★

If you prefer not to deep-fry, place the
marinated chicken under a hot grill for
15–20 minutes, turning occasionally, until
cooked through and starting to char.

I remember going to watch Twenty Thousand Leagues Under the Sea *when I was about eight. It was evening and we stopped to have an early supper. I had Chicken Pattice, an example of the Portuguese influence in modern-day India. It was a pie made from buttery, flaky pastry filled with the most delicious spicy chicken filling. I don't remember the movie, but I do remember those delectable pies. After many attempts, I have achieved a satisfying re-creation of those hearty crowd-pleasers. They never last long once they have been taken out of the oven!*

CHICKEN MANCHURIAN
HAND PIES

MAKES 12

1 TABLESPOON VEGETABLE OIL

1 RED ONION, FINELY CHOPPED

1 SMALL TOMATO, FINELY CHOPPED

1 TEASPOON FINELY GRATED GINGER

2 TEASPOONS MINCED GARLIC

300G CHICKEN THIGH FILLETS, DICED

¼ CUP KETCHUP (TOMATO SAUCE)

1 TEASPOON WHITE VINEGAR

1 TEASPOON SOY SAUCE

½ TEASPOON GARAM MASALA

¼ TEASPOON WHITE PEPPER

¼ CUP SLICED SPRING ONIONS

1 TEASPOON CORNFLOUR

3 SHEETS FROZEN PUFF PASTRY, THAWED

1 EGG WHISKED WITH 1 TABLESPOON WATER

SESAME SEEDS

LUSTY CHUTNEY (PAGE 85), TO SERVE

Heat the oil in a frying pan on medium heat. Add the onion, tomato, ginger and garlic. Sauté for a few minutes, until the onion is soft. Increase the heat to high and add the chicken. Sauté for a few minutes until the chicken starts to brown. Reduce the heat to low. Add the ketchup, vinegar, soy sauce, garam masala and white pepper. Season with salt and add the spring onions. Cook for a few minutes, until the chicken is cooked through. Mix the cornflour with ¼ cup (60ml) water and stir into the chicken mixture. Cook until the sauce thickens. Remove from the heat and cool completely.

Preheat the oven to 220°C and line a baking tray with baking paper. Cut each pastry sheet into four squares. Place ¼ cup of the chicken mixture a little off-centre into one square. Wet the edges of the pastry with water and gently fold over to enclose the filling. Crimp down and seal the edges with your fingers. Repeat with all the pastry and filling.

Brush the tops and sides of each pie with the egg wash. Sprinkle some sesame seeds on top and bake for about 18 minutes, or until the pies are puffed and golden. Serve with Lusty Chutney (page 85).

★ ★ ★

PULLED PORK
BANH MI

PULLED PORK

2KG PORK SHOULDER

2 TABLESPOONS SALT

2 TABLESPOONS GARLIC PASTE

1 TABLESPOON CHINESE FIVE SPICE POWDER

DRIZZLE OF OLIVE OIL

ASIAN SAUCE

2 TABLESPOONS SESAME OIL

4 GARLIC CLOVES, MINCED

1 CUP (250ML) KETCHUP (TOMATO SAUCE)

½ CUP (125ML) HOISIN SAUCE

½ CUP (125ML) SHAOXING WINE

BANH MI

8 VIETNAMESE BAGUETTES (OR LONG BREAD ROLLS)

1 AVOCADO, HALVED, SEED REMOVED

2 LARGE TOMATOES, THINLY SLICED

2 LEBANESE CUCUMBERS, THINLY SLICED LENGTHWISE

1 RED ONION, HALVED AND THINLY SLICED

1 LARGE CARROT, JULIENNED

FEW STALKS OF SPRING ONION, WHITE BITS TRIMMED

1 LARGE RED CHILLI, THINLY SLICED

FEW SPRIGS OF CORIANDER

To cook the pulled pork, preheat the oven to 200°C. Place the pork in a large roasting dish. Rub all over with the salt, garlic paste and five spice powder. Drizzle generously with oil and rub it in. Cover the pork with two layers of aluminium foil, tucking the foil under the rim of the roasting tray and making sure there are no gaps to let air in. Roast for 4 hours. Remove from the oven and rest for 30 minutes. Using two forks, gently shred the meat. It should be tender and come apart easily. Place the shredded meat in a large bowl.

To make the sauce, place all the ingredients in a small saucepan. Bring to the boil and remove from the heat. Add the hot sauce to the shredded pork and mix well.

To assemble the banh mi, slice each baguette in half. Spread avocado onto the base of each one. Top with slices of tomato, cucumber and onion, then carrot, spring onion, chilli and coriander. Add a thick layer of the saucy pork. Top with the other half of the baguettes.

★ ★ ★

This is a fantastic make-ahead tart for a day out in the sun enjoying a picnic or camping. A thick slice topped with salad greens would make the most luxurious lunch at work.

SOUR CREAM & ROAST VEGGIE TART

SERVES 6

2 SMALL EGGPLANTS, CUT INTO 2CM SLICES

1 LARGE SWEET POTATO, COARSELY DICED

1 LARGE RED ONION, THICKLY SLICED

¼ CUP (60ML) OLIVE OIL

2 SHEETS FROZEN SHORTCRUST PASTRY, THAWED

1 CUP (240G) FRESH RICOTTA (FROM THE DELI)

1 CUP (240G) SOUR CREAM

2 EGGS

7–8 FRESH THYME SPRIGS, LEAVES PICKED

8–10 CHERRY TOMATOES, HALVED

SALAD GREENS, TO SERVE

Preheat the oven to 230°C and line a baking tray with baking paper. Combine the eggplant, sweet potato and onion in a large bowl. Season with salt and pepper, drizzle with the oil and toss to coat. Spread onto the prepared tray. Roast for 25–30 minutes or until they are golden and starting to brown. Remove from oven and set aside to cool.

Reduce the oven to 180°C and grease a 38cm x 12cm (base measurement) rectangular loose-based tart tin. Place the two sheets of pastry together, overlapping by about 1cm, and press the join to seal and make one long sheet. Ease the pastry into the tart tin, pressing gently in the corners. Make sure there is excess pastry hanging over the edges (it will shrink during cooking). Line the pastry with a large sheet of baking paper and fill with pie weights (or raw rice or dried beans), to weigh the pastry down. Bake for 30 minutes. Remove from the oven and carefully remove the paper and weights. Bake for a further 10 minutes, until the pastry turns a beautiful shade of gold. Set aside to cool.

Scatter some of the roast veggies into the pastry case. In a large bowl, whisk together the ricotta, sour cream, eggs and half the thyme. Season with salt and freshly ground black pepper. Gently spoon the ricotta mixture over the roast veggies. Dot the ricotta mixture with the cherry tomatoes, remaining roast veggies and thyme.

Bake for about 30 minutes, until the filling has set and the top is starting to brown evenly. Set aside for 10 minutes, then break off excess overhanging pastry. Serve with salad greens.

★ ★ ★

You could make this in a 24cm round tart tin if you like.

When I lived in Mumbai (then known as Bombay), street snacks were a way of life. Sandwich-wallahs would pedal their mobile carts carrying sandwiches that groaned under layers of vegetables, salads and chutneys, and perhaps a secret ingredient unique to the peddler. They all had one thing in common: boiled potatoes and a fragrant green chutney. This sandwich is a lifesaver when I don't have time to cook lunch.

BOMBAY
SANDWICH

SERVES 2

4 SLICES GRAIN BREAD, BUTTERED

2 SMALL LEBANESE CUCUMBERS, THINLY SLICED

2 SMALL TOMATOES, THINLY SLICED

½ CUP CORIANDER CHUTNEY (SEE BELOW)

2 SMALL POTATOES, BOILED, PEELED AND THINLY SLICED

A DRIZZLE OF YOUR FAVOURITE CHILLI SAUCE

½ CUP MIXED SPROUTED BEANS (SEE PAGE 123)

½ CUP MICRO HERBS (I USED HOMEGROWN MUSTARD GREENS)

CORIANDER CHUTNEY

1 BUNCH OF CORIANDER (ROOTS DISCARDED, LEAVES AND STALKS WASHED AND CHOPPED)

1 TABLESPOON CHOPPED FRESH GINGER

1 GARLIC CLOVE

HANDFUL OF MINT LEAVES

JUICE OF ½ LEMON

1 TABLESPOON RAW SUGAR

1 TEASPOON SALT

¼ CUP ROASTED PEANUTS

1 SMALL RED CHILLI, ROUGHLY CHOPPED

Lay two slices of bread on a cutting board. Arrange the sliced cucumber onto the bread slices, and top with the sliced tomato. Drop generous dollops of the coriander chutney onto the tomato slices. Top with the sliced potato, and drizzle generously with chilli sauce. Season with freshly ground black pepper. Top with the sprouted beans, then the micro herbs. Cover with the remaining bread slices, and serve.

To make the coriander chutney, place all the ingredients into a food processor or blender with ¼ cup (60ml) water. Process until smooth. Store in a lidded glass jar in the fridge for up to 3 days.

If you don't have micro herbs, snow pea sprouts or alfalfa sprouts work well. They are available in your supermarket.

★ ★ ★

ZESTY CHORIZO & CHICKPEA
TAPAS

SERVES 2

1 TABLESPOON OLIVE OIL

1 SMALL RED ONION, FINELY CHOPPED

2 GARLIC CLOVES, MINCED

1 BAY LEAF

2 CHORIZO SAUSAGES, SLICED INTO 1CM DISCS

½ CUP (125ML) BEER

1 CUP (190G) CANNED CHICKPEAS, RINSED AND DRAINED

1 TABLESPOON SWEET PAPRIKA

1 TEASPOON SMOKED PAPRIKA

½ TEASPOON DRIED OREGANO

1 TABLESPOON BALSAMIC VINEGAR

2 TABLESPOONS TOMATO PASTE

CRUSTY BREAD, TO SERVE

Heat the oil in a frying pan on medium heat. Sauté the onion and garlic until golden brown. Add the bay leaf and chorizo. Sauté for a few minutes, then add the beer and bring to a simmer.

Cook for a few minutes, until the beer is reduced by half. Stir in the chickpeas, sweet and smoked paprika, oregano, balsamic vinegar, and tomato paste. Simmer for a few minutes until everything is well combined, then season with salt to taste. Serve hot with crusty bread.

★ ★ ★

Sprinkle the finished dish with a little fresh oregano if you have some.

SWEET POTATO & PEPITA
BURGERS

SERVES 6

450G SWEET POTATO, PEELED AND CHOPPED

6 WHOLE (UNPEELED) GARLIC CLOVES

SPRAY COOKING OIL

1½ SLICES WHOLEMEAL BREAD, CRUSTS ON, TORN

400G CAN RED KIDNEY BEANS, RINSED AND DRAINED

1½ TEASPOONS SMOKED PAPRIKA

2 TEASPOONS SALT

¼ CUP (30G) PECANS

½ CUP (75G) PEPITAS

OLIVE OIL, FOR FRYING

Preheat the oven to 200°C and line a baking tray with baking paper. Place the sweet potato and garlic onto the baking tray, and spray with oil. Bake for about 30 minutes, until soft and lightly browned. Set aside to cool completely. Squeeze the garlic cloves out of their skins.

Reduce the oven temperature to 180°C. Place the sweet potato, garlic, bread, red kidney beans, paprika, salt and pecans into a food processor and process until it forms a coarse paste.

Using your hands, shape the mixture into six patties about 10cm in diameter and 2cm thick. Place the pepitas into a wide shallow dish and, working one at a time, place a patty into the dish and turn to coat with pepitas. Repeat with the remaining patties.

Heat about 2 tablespoons of oil in a large frying pan on medium heat, and cook 2–3 patties for 5–6 minutes on each side until golden. Repeat with the remaining patties.

Place the cooked patties onto a baking tray lined with baking paper. Bake for 15 minutes until browned all over.

These patties make a filling little snack. They are also great as vegetarian burgers, sandwiched in grain bread with salad greens and fresh chutney. Cooked patties can be frozen for up to a month. Try adding in a couple of slices of roasted beetroot before processing for a healthy (and tasty!) variation.

★ ★ ★

TEA-SMOKED FRIED RICE
WITH **PRAWNS**

On the eve of a road trip, I make a wok-full of this rice and pack it away in lunch boxes for the morning. It is usually our first meal of the day when we make a rest stop on our adventure. It has such an amazing depth of flavour from the tea that it doesn't need anything other than chilli sauce for an extra bite. It goes delightfully with Nick's Chilli Chicken on page 140.

TEASPOON PEANUT OIL	1 SMALL CARROT, FINELY DICED
CUP (220G) JASMINE RICE	½ CUP SLICED, FINELY CHOPPED CABBAGE
TEA BAG (STRONG, SMOKY TEA LIKE LAPSANG SOUCHANG), PAPER AND STRING REMOVED	1 TABLESPOON WHITE VINEGAR
TABLESPOONS PEANUT OIL, EXTRA	1 TEASPOON SOY SAUCE
EGGS, LIGHTLY BEATEN	1 TEASPOON SALT
½ CUP (75G) FROZEN PEAS	¼ CUP SLICED SPRING ONIONS
00G FROZEN COOKED AND PEELED PRAWNS, THAWED	HANDFUL OF CHOPPED CORIANDER LEAVES

Heat the teaspoon of oil in a heavy-bottomed saucepan on low heat. Add the rice and tea bag. Sauté for 5 minutes, stirring constantly. Add 1⅓ cups (330ml) cold water. Cook for a minute, then remove the tea bag. Increase the heat to medium and cook for 8 minutes, covered, until the rice has absorbed the water. Remove from heat and set aside to cool completely.

In a wok, heat one tablespoon of extra oil on high heat. Add the eggs. Cook for a minute and then chop the cooked egg up with a spatula. Move the egg to one side of the wok. Add the remaining oil in the middle of the wok. Add the peas, prawns, carrot and cabbage to the hot oil. Stir-fry on high heat for a minute, mixing the egg with the veggies.

Add the vinegar, soy sauce, salt and cooled rice. Stir-fry for a few minutes, turning constantly, until the rice is heated through and everything is mixed well.

Remove from the heat and serve hot, garnished with spring onions and coriander.

★ ★ ★

Frozen prawns release water when cooked. It is important to thaw them and drain the excess liquid. If you don't have time to thaw them, microwave them in a bowl on high for one minute. Squeeze and drain all water out, and pat dry with paper towels before adding to the wok.

This is pure comfort in a deep dish. It is a perfect lunch on a cool, windy day. I often make a vegetarian version by substituting bacon with finely chopped eggplant, but this one is loved profusely by my boys at home.

PUMPKIN & BACON
MAC & CHEESE

SERVES 4

1½ CUPS COOKED MACARONI

2 TABLESPOONS BUTTER

1 CUP FINELY CHOPPED PUMPKIN

1 CUP FINELY CHOPPED BACON

2 GARLIC CLOVES, MINCED

¼ CUP (40G) PLAIN FLOUR

1 BAY LEAF

2 CUPS (500ML) MILK

¼ CUP (20G) GRATED PARMESAN CHEESE, PLUS EXTRA TO SERVE

¼ CUP (25G) GRATED CHEDDAR CHEESE

4 SPRIGS OF THYME, LEAVES PICKED

Preheat the oven to 180°C. Place the cooked macaroni into a large ovenproof casserole dish (about 24cm diameter and 6cm deep). Set aside.

Melt 1 tablespoon of the butter in a saucepan on medium heat. Add the pumpkin, bacon and garlic. Sauté for 10 minutes, until the pumpkin and bacon start becoming golden. Remove from the heat and add the pumpkin mixture to the macaroni.

Wipe out the saucepan. Melt the remaining butter in the saucepan on low heat. Add the flour and toast for a few minutes until it becomes a shade darker. Add the bay leaf and then gradually pour in the milk while stirring constantly to remove lumps. Cook, stirring, for a few minutes until the sauce thickens and is smooth. Remove from heat.

Add the parmesan, cheddar and thyme to the milk mixture and season with salt and freshly ground black pepper. Mix well. Add mixture to the macaroni mixture, and fold together until evenly combined. Bake for 30 minutes until golden and bubbling on top.

Serve sprinkled with extra grated parmesan cheese.

★ ★ ★

You'll need to cook about 1 cup raw macaroni to yield 1½ cups cooked.

Cooking daal may seem intimidating, but this basic recipe reveals how quickly and easily it can be made into a nourishing meal. Do not be afraid of the quantity of water stipulated. The key is to cook the daal on a high heat until the lentils are cooked and fluffy and then simmer on a low heat to let the flavours develop and to achieve the consistency you want. Crispy kale is worth a go, but you could also just stir the kale into the daal at the very end. It can be substituted with spinach or silverbeet.

KALE DAAL
FRY

SERVES 4

1 TABLESPOON BUTTER

1/2 TEASPOON MUSTARD SEEDS

1/2 TEASPOON NIGELLA SEEDS

1 BAY LEAF

1/2 CINNAMON STICK

1 CUP (190G) RED LENTILS

1/4 CUP (50G) BROWN LENTILS

1 TEASPOON FINELY GRATED GINGER PASTE

1 TEASPOON MINCED GARLIC

1 LARGE TOMATO, DICED

1 1/4 TEASPOONS SALT

1/4 TEASPOON GROUND TURMERIC

1 TABLESPOON OLIVE OIL

3 LARGE KALE LEAVES, STEMS TRIMMED AND LEAVES CHOPPED

STEAMED RICE OR FLATBREADS, TO SERVE

SLICED RED CHILLIES TO GARNISH, OPTIONAL

Heat the butter in a saucepan on medium heat. Add the mustard seeds, nigella seeds, bay leaf, cinnamon and lentils. Sauté for a minute, until the seeds start crackling and the lentils are glazed with butter.

Add the ginger, garlic and tomato, and stir-fry for a few seconds. Add the salt, turmeric and 4 cups (1 litre) water. Bring to the boil, then reduce the heat to medium and simmer uncovered for 20 minutes. Stir occasionally and check to make sure it still has water and isn't sticking. Reduce the heat to low, add another 1/2 cup (125ml) water, cover and cook for another 5 minutes, until lentils are tender. Remove from the heat and set aside.

Heat the olive oil in a large frying pan on medium heat. Add the kale and sauté for a few seconds, until leaves are glazed with oil and starting to become crisp. Remove from the heat.

Top the daal with the crispy kale leaves, and serve hot with steamed rice or flatbreads. Top with sliced chillies if you like.

★ ★ ★

I often used to cook this filling dish when I was first discovering the joys of a plant-based style of eating. I would buy a big tub of mixed sprouts and have a piping hot meal within minutes of reaching home. Leftovers were packed away for the next day's lunch. Nowadays, I grow my own sprouts because I love experimenting with different legumes in the mix. It is also cheaper and you can make huge quantities that can be frozen easily. You can also make this dish with canned chickpeas or fresh stir-fry vegetables.

SPICY MOROCCAN
SPROUTS

1 TABLESPOON OLIVE OIL

1 LARGE RED ONION, FINELY CHOPPED

2 GARLIC CLOVES, MINCED

3 CUPS MIXED SPROUTS (SEE PAGE 123)

5 TEASPOONS MOROCCAN SPICE MIX

SALT TO TASTE

400G CAN CHOPPED TOMATOES

LEMON WEDGES, CORIANDER LEAVES AND
FLATBREAD, TO SERVE

MOROCCAN SPICE MIX (MAKES ABOUT A CUP)

5 TABLESPOONS GROUND CUMIN

5 TABLESPOONS GROUND CORIANDER

1 TABLESPOON GROUND CINNAMON

1 TABLESPOON GROUND ALLSPICE

1 TABLESPOON GROUND PAPRIKA

1 TEASPOON GROUND GINGER

1/2 TEASPOON GROUND NUTMEG

1/4 TEASPOON GROUND TURMERIC

Heat the oil in a large saucepan on high heat.
Add the onion and garlic. Sauté for a few
minutes, until soft. Add the sprouts and spice
mix. Cook for 3 minutes. Add the tomatoes and
1 cup (250ml) water. Mix well. Reduce the heat
to low and simmer uncovered for 20 minutes.
Season with salt to taste.

Serve hot with lemon wedges, coriander leaves
and flatbreads.

To make the Moroccan spice mix, combine all
the ingredients in a dry bowl. Mix well. Store
in an airtight container in a cool corner of your
pantry for a month or two. Use as required.

★ ★ ★

HOW TO GROW
SPROUTS

MAKES 4 CUPS

Sprouts are versatile, delicious and bursting with goodness. Stir them through salads, curries and stir-fries. Layer them in sandwiches. Pickle them. Use them as a garnish. They're also super-easy to grow in your own kitchen. You can sprout chickpeas, peas, mung beans, split peas, lentils, quinoa, sunflower seeds, chia seeds, sesame seeds, almonds, peanuts, hazel nuts and amaranth. Choose your favourites and get soaking!

1. Layer your legumes in a 1 litre wide-mouth glass jar.

2. Pour warm water over your legumes, enough to completely submerge them and allow room to grow.

3. Soak your legumes uncovered for 4–6 hours.

4. After the first soak, secure a folded paper towel or muslin cloth with a rubber band over the mouth of the jar. This will allow the air inside the jar to breathe and not get mouldy.

5. Invert the jar over a sink or basin and drain all the water away.

6. Pour fresh warm water over the legumes and soak them for another 4–6 hours.

7. Make sure the second soak is with the paper towel or muslin cloth firmly attached to the mouth of the jar.

8. At the end of the second soak, the water will have been almost completely absorbed and the legumes will have doubled in size.

9. Rinse the legumes in cold water and drain the water completely. Secure the mouth with the paper towel/muslin cloth and rest for a few hours. Perform this rinse twice daily.

10. On the third day, your legumes will have sprouted and be ready to eat. If you desire longer sprouts, you can continue rinsing and draining twice every day for another couple of days. This is important to keep the legumes slime-free and to stop the growth of mould.

> Ready-to-eat sprouts can be used straight away or stored in the fridge for up to a week in a lidded box. They can be frozen for up to a month. To make 4 cups, start with 1½ cups of raw sprouts: for example, ¼ cup each of chickpeas, green peas and brown lentils plus ½ cup of mung beans.

My fascination with the famous Japanese pancake made with cabbage started when I was living in Singapore and I discovered a thin-crust okonomiyaki pizza. When I first moved to Sydney I was completely enamoured of the Japanese pancakes being sold at markets every weekend. I would scour new markets to sample yet another okonomiyaki stall. Here I have created a wholesome version and used a mix of green and purple cabbage for added colour.

WHOLEMEAL JAPANESE PANCAKES

SERVES 2

½ CUP (80G) WHOLEMEAL PLAIN FLOUR

1 CUP FINELY SLICED PURPLE CABBAGE

1 CUP FINELY SLICED GREEN CABBAGE

½ CUP GRATED POTATO

½ CUP SLICED SPRING ONIONS

4 EGGS

½ TEASPOON SALT

1 TABLESPOON SOY SAUCE

1 TABLESPOON MIRIN

OLIVE OIL, FOR FRYING

SESAME SEEDS, TO SPRINKLE

JAPANESE MAYONNAISE, BARBECUE SAUCE, SRIRACHA SAUCE (OPTIONAL) TO SERVE

Combine the flour, cabbage, potato, spring onions, egg, salt, soy sauce and mirin in a large bowl. Mix well.

Heat a little oil in a medium frying pan on medium-low heat. Spoon half the batter into the frying pan. Gently spread to a 12cm round and sprinkle with sesame seeds. Cook for 3–5 minutes, until bubbles start appearing on the surface. Using a wide spatula, flip the pancake gently and cook the other side until golden. Repeat with the remaining batter to make two pancakes.

To serve, place a pancake on a plate. Squeeze the mayonnaise in a criss-cross pattern, followed by a layer of barbecue sauce and a layer of Sriracha sauce (if using) in the same pattern.

★ ★ ★

BEETROOT LEAF & YOGHURT
FLATBREADS

FLATBREAD

2 CUPS (300G) PLAIN FLOUR

½ TEASPOON BAKING POWDER

½ TEASPOON DRY YEAST

PINCH OF SALT

3 TABLESPOONS GREEK YOGHURT

2 TABLESPOONS OLIVE OIL

FILLING

8-10 BEETROOT LEAVES AND STEMS

2 TABLESPOONS OLIVE OIL, PLUS EXTRA TO COOK THE FILLED BREADS

1 RED ONION, FINELY CHOPPED

2 GARLIC CLOVES, FINELY CHOPPED

¼ CUP (40G) PINE NUTS, TOASTED

1 TEASPOON GROUND CUMIN

1 TEASPOON SMOKED PAPRIKA

100G FETA CHEESE, CRUMBLED

To make the flatbreads, combine the flour, baking powder, yeast and salt in a large bowl. Add the yoghurt and ½ cup (125ml) water, and mix with a wooden spoon to make a dough. Turn onto a flour-dusted surface and knead for a few minutes until smooth. Return to the bowl. Cover with a tea towel and set in a warm corner of your kitchen for about 30 minutes to prove, until doubled in size.

Add the olive oil to the dough and knead until smooth. Cover and set aside for another 30 minutes. Divide the dough into 4 balls. Roll each dough ball into 20cm rounds that are about 5mm thick.

To make the filling, wash the beetroot leaves and stems. Pat dry and chop finely. Heat the olive oil in a large frying pan on medium heat. Cook the onion and garlic for about 5 minutes until softened. Add the beetroot leaves and stems, pine nuts, cumin, paprika and a pinch of salt. Add ½ cup (125ml) water and cook for 10 minutes on low heat until the beetroot leaves start to wilt. Increase the heat to high and cook for a minute or two, to dry up the water, stirring to avoid sticking.

To assemble and cook the flatbreads, heat a little oil in a heavy-bottomed frying pan on medium-low heat. Add 1 flatbread. Top with half the beetroot mixture and half the crumbled feta. Place another flatbread on top and press down around the edges to seal. Cook for 2 minutes until the filling is warm, cheese has melted and flatbread is toasted. Carefully flip the flatbread over and cook the other side for 2 minutes. Drizzle oil around the side to toast it.

Repeat the process with the remaining flatbreads and filling. Place cooked flatbread on a serving board and wait for it to cool before cutting it into quarters. Eat straight away with salad greens and hot sauce, or wrap each quarter in wax paper and take along in a box for a great picnic snack.

This is a flavourful take on gözleme, the traditional Turkish stuffed flatbread, and it is fun to make. It is a great way to use up nutritious beetroot leaves. The yoghurt flatbreads are super-easy and delicious with other recipes like the Speedy Egg Curry on page 138.

MUNCHIES

THAI-SPICED LIME
ALMONDS

MAKES 2 CUPS

2 TABLESPOONS VEGETABLE OIL

6 MEDIUM KAFFIR LIME LEAVES, FINELY CHOPPED

1½ TEASPOONS DRIED RED CHILLI FLAKES

1 TEASPOON GARLIC GRANULES

1 TEASPOON SALT

¼ TEASPOON SWEET PAPRIKA

2 CUPS (360G) RAW ALMONDS

4 WHOLE KAFFIR LIME LEAVES, EXTRA, ROUGHLY TORN

Heat the oil in a large frying pan on medium heat. Add the lime leaves, chilli flakes, garlic, salt, paprika and almonds. Sauté for a few minutes, tossing constantly to coat the almonds with the spices. Reduce the heat to low and continue toasting the almonds for 25–30 minutes, stirring occasionally, until fragrant and toasted. Keep an eye on them so they cook evenly. Stir through the torn lime leaves. Remove from the heat and cool completely.

Store in an airtight container for up to 2 weeks.

BAKED SPINACH CRISPIES

MAKES 30

- 20G PLAIN FLOUR
- 30G RYE FLOUR
- ¼ CUP (60ML) OLIVE OIL
- ¼ CUP (20G) GRATED PARMESAN CHEESE
- TEASPOON CUMIN SEEDS
- TEASPOON SESAME SEEDS
- TEASPOON SALT
- ½ TEASPOON SWEET PAPRIKA
- ¼ TEASPOON GROUND CINNAMON
- ½ CUP FINELY CHOPPED SPINACH LEAVES

Preheat the oven to 180°C and line a baking tray with baking paper.

Place all the ingredients into a bowl with ½ cup (125ml) water and knead for a few minutes to form a stiff but pliable dough.

Roll the dough out into a thin rectangular shape (2.5mm thick). Using a fluted pastry cutter, cut the dough into rectangles about 3cm x 3cm. Place the rectangles onto the prepared tray, and prick them several times with a fork.

Bake for 12–15 minutes until golden and crispy. Cool completely and store in an airtight container for up to a week.

★ ★ ★

3. WHOLEMEAL ROSEMARY COOKIES

MAKES 36

- ⅔ CUP (160ML) RICE BRAN OIL
- FINELY GRATED RIND OF 1 ORANGE
- ⅔ CUP (160ML) FRESHLY SQUEEZED ORANGE JUICE
- 1½ CUPS (240G) WHOLEMEAL PLAIN FLOUR
- ½ TEASPOON BAKING POWDER
- 1 CUP (200G) BROWN SUGAR
- PINCH OF SALT
- ⅔ CUP (60G) ROLLED OATS
- ⅔ CUP (60G) DESICCATED COCONUT
- 2 TABLESPOONS FRESH ROSEMARY LEAVES, FINELY CHOPPED
- ⅔ CUP (120G) RAISINS, FINELY CHOPPED
- 1 CUP (100G) ROASTED WALNUTS, COARSELY CHOPPED

Preheat the oven to 180°C and line a baking tray with baking paper. Whisk the oil, orange rind, orange juice, flour, baking powder, sugar and a pinch of salt with electric beaters until combined. Add the remaining ingredients and mix well with a wooden spoon.

Take tablespoons of mixture and form small flattened rounds with your palms. Place onto the prepared tray a few centimetres apart. Bake for 20 minutes. Remove from the oven and cool on wire racks. Store in an airtight jar when completely cooled.

★ ★ ★

SUPPER CLUB

Suppers are a time to kick back and relax with great company, happy chatter and delicious food. Whether it is for a meal for two, a party of six or a campsite of twelve, here you will find something exciting for all occasions. Clever pies, multi-tasking curries, adventurous roasts, fun stir-fries and wholesome pastas take the fuss out of night-time meals.

THIRSTIES

Cold-Pressed Ice Coffee
Green Mango Cooler
Iced Lemon Tea

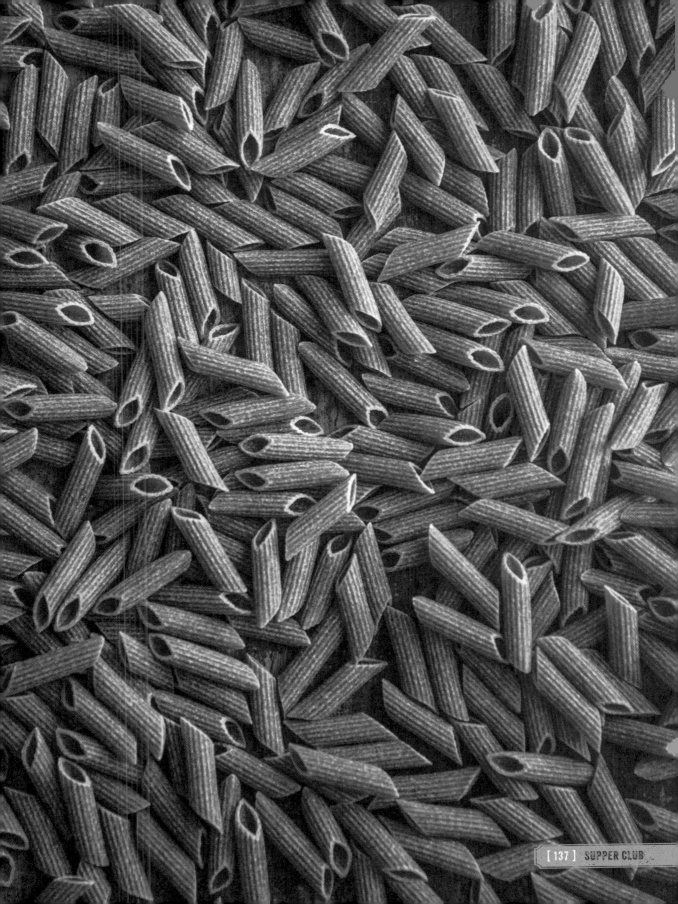

SPEEDY
EGG CURRY

SERVES 4

2 TABLESPOONS BUTTER

1 LARGE BAY LEAF

1 LARGE RED ONION, FINELY CHOPPED

1 TABLESPOON GARLIC PASTE

1 TEASPOON GINGER PASTE

400G CAN CRUSHED TOMATOES

1/4 CUP (60ML) TOMATO PASSATA

2 TABLESPOONS SUGAR

1 TABLESPOON GROUND CUMIN

1 TABLESPOON GROUND CORIANDER

1 TEASPOON GARAM MASALA

1/2 TEASPOON GROUND CINNAMON

1/2 TEASPOON GROUND CARDAMOM

1/2 TEASPOON TURMERIC

1/2 TSP GROUND CHILLI (OR RED CHILLI FLAKES)

1/4 CUP (60ML) CREAM

SALT, TO TASTE

8 BOILED EGGS, PEELED AND HALVED

HANDFUL OF CORIANDER LEAVES, TO SERVE

SLICED RED ONION, TO SERVE

Melt the butter in a saucepan on medium heat, and add the bay leaf. Sauté for a few seconds until fragrant. Add the onion, garlic paste and ginger paste. Sauté until the onion is soft.

Add the tomatoes and passata, reduce the heat to low and sauté for a few minutes until the mixture becomes a shade darker. Add the sugar, cumin, coriander, garam masala, cinnamon, cardamom, turmeric and chilli. Cook for a few minutes, stirring to combine. Stir in 1 cup (250ml) water.

Cover and bring to a simmer. Cook over low heat for about 25 minutes until fragrant and a nice rich shade of red. Stir through the cream, cook for another minute and remove from heat. Season with salt to taste. Place the boiled eggs into the curry sauce and serve hot, garnished with coriander leaves and sliced onion.

★ ★ ★

This tasty curry sauce quickly comes together with pantry ingredients. You can swap the eggs for chicken, paneer, chickpeas or even a combination of all three.

One year we bought several different varieties of chilli plants from the nursery. Later we had a bumper crop and Nick invented this recipe. It is his most requested recipe – by me! If you love a good hit of heat in your food, you must make this. You can also tone it down by adding less chilli, of course.

NICK'S
CHILLI CHICKEN

SERVES 4

2 TABLESPOONS VEGETABLE OIL

2 TEASPOONS GINGER PASTE

2 TEASPOONS GARLIC PASTE

500G CHICKEN THIGH FILLETS, CUT INTO 2.5CM PIECES

1 LONG GREEN CHILLI, DESEEDED AND SLICED

1 SMALL RED CAPSICUM, DICED

¼ CUP CHOPPED SPRING ONIONS

1 CUP (250ML) CHICKEN STOCK

1 TEASPOON VINEGAR

1 TEASPOON SOY SAUCE

4 TEASPOONS CORNFLOUR

¼ CUP CHOPPED SPRING ONION TOPS (GREEN PART), TO GARNISH

STEAMED RICE AND SLICED CUCUMBER, TO SERVE

Heat 1 tablespoon of the oil in a saucepan on high heat. Add 1 teaspoon each of the ginger and garlic pastes. Add the chicken and sauté for a few minutes, until browned. Remove from heat, take the chicken out of the pan using a slotted spoon and place into a bowl.

Return the pan to the heat and add the other tablespoon of oil. Add the remaining ginger and garlic pastes, chilli, capsicum and spring onions. Season with salt. Sauté for a minute, then add the chicken stock, vinegar and soy sauce. Return the chicken to the pan.

Reduce the heat to low and simmer for 3–4 minutes. Combine the cornflour with ¼ cup (60ml) water and stir in. Cook until the sauce boils and thickens.

Remove from the heat and garnish with spring onion tops. Serve with hot steamed rice and cucumber.

★ ★ ★

GRILLED SALMON
WITH PEACH & GRAPEFRUIT RELISH

SERVES 2

This is an inviting light summer dish with lovely clean flavours. Fish doesn't take long to cook and grilling it is super easy. You can substitute salmon with a firm white fish like ling or trout.

2 LARGE SALMON STEAKS, SKIN ON
(ABOUT 250G EACH)

JUICE OF 1 LEMON

1 LARGE PEACH, PITTED AND FINELY CHOPPED

1 LARGE GRAPEFRUIT, PEELED, PITH REMOVED
AND ROUGHLY CHOPPED

1 SMALL RED ONION, FINELY CHOPPED

1 TABLESPOON OLIVE OIL

JUICE OF ½ LEMON

1 TEASPOON SUGAR

¼ TEASPOON SALT

¼ CUP CHOPPED FRESH MINT

¼ CUP CHOPPED FRESH PARSLEY

FRESHLY GROUND BLACK PEPPER

SPRAY COOKING OIL

LEMON WEDGES, TO SERVE

Place the salmon steaks into a shallow bowl. Drizzle with the juice from 1 lemon, and season with salt and freshly ground black pepper. Set aside in the fridge for 30 minutes.

To make the relish, place the peach, grapefruit, onion, olive oil, lemon juice, sugar, salt, mint and parsley into a large bowl. Season with freshly ground black pepper and toss to mix well.

Heat a chargrill pan on high heat. Spray the salmon steaks liberally with cooking oil and place onto the hot grill. Grill for 6–10 minutes each side until skin is crispy and the salmon is still a tiny bit pink in the middle. Place the salmon onto serving plates a plate, top with the relish and serve with lemon wedges.

★ ★ ★

MATTAR PANEER PIE
WITH NAAN TOP

SERVES 6

This is a conversation-starting vegetarian main. A pie with a twist! An aromatic golden curry is topped with naan dough and baked in the oven. You can also cook the curry by itself.

2 LARGE TOMATOES, COARSELY CHOPPED	1 TABLESPOON SUGAR
2.5CM PIECE OF GINGER	½ TEASPOON SALT
A BIG HANDFUL OF CORIANDER LEAVES	½ TEASPOON GROUND CHILLI
1 SMALL GREEN CHILLI	¼ TEASPOON GROUND TURMERIC
1 TABLESPOON GHEE OR BUTTER	¼ CUP (70G) YOGHURT
1 BAY LEAF	NAAN DOUGH (SEE PAGE 146)
1 CUP (300G) TOMATO PASSATA	MELTED BUTTER, TO BRUSH
500G PANEER, CUBED	NIGELLA SEEDS AND FINELY CHOPPED HERBS
1½ CUPS (225G) FROZEN PEAS	(SUCH AS THYME OR CORIANDER),
1 TABLESPOON GROUND CUMIN	TO SPRINKLE

Place the tomatoes, ginger, coriander, chilli and 1 cup (250ml) water in the jug of a blender and blend until smooth.

Heat the ghee in a large heavy-bottomed saucepan on medium heat. Add the bay leaf and sauté for a few seconds, until fragrant. Add the tomato mixture and the passata. Sauté for a few minutes until it turns a shade darker. Add the paneer, peas, cumin, sugar, salt, chilli and turmeric.

Reduce the heat to low, cover and simmer for 30 minutes. Stir through yoghurt, increase heat to high and cook for a minute or two until creamy. Remove from the heat and pour into a 20cm round (base measurement), 6cm deep pie dish. Cool completely.

Preheat the oven to 200°C. Divide the naan dough into two portions. You only need half for this recipe, so store the remaining dough in a container in the fridge for up to 2 days.

Roll out the dough to a round, about 26cm in diameter. Place the rolled dough gently over the cooled filling, letting it hang over the edges of the pie dish. Press down the edges to seal lightly. Brush the top with melted butter and sprinkle with nigella seeds and finely chopped herbs.

Bake the pie for 20–25 minutes, until the naan topping is cooked and golden.

★ ★ ★

HOW TO MAKE
NAAN

MAKES 4

1 TEASPOON DRY YEAST

1 TEASPOON CASTER SUGAR

2 CUPS (300G) PLAIN FLOUR

½ TEASPOON BAKING POWDER

PINCH OF SALT

½ CUP (125ML) MILK

½ CUP (140G) GREEK YOGHURT

1 TABLESPOON OLIVE OIL

MELTED BUTTER, TO BRUSH

NIGELLA SEEDS, TO SPRINKLE

Place the yeast, sugar and ¼ cup (60ml) warm water into a small
bowl. Set aside in a warm place for 10 minutes, until the mixture
becomes frothy.

Combine the flour, baking powder and salt in a large bowl. Make a
well in the centre. Add milk, yoghurt and yeast mixture to the well.
Mix gently with a wooden spoon until it starts coming together. Turn
onto a flour-dusted surface and knead for a few minutes until smooth.
Return to the bowl. Cover with a clean tea towel and set in a warm corner
of your kitchen for about 30 minutes to prove, until doubled in size.

Add the olive oil to the dough and knead in until smooth. Cover and
set aside for another 30 minutes.

Divide the dough into four balls. Dust a clean surface with flour and roll
a portion of dough into a teardrop shape. Stretch the shape gently with
your fingers to get a rustic-looking naan that is less than 5mm thick.

Heat a heavy-bottomed frying pan with a lid on high heat. Brush one
side of the naan with water. Place the naan, water side down, into the
frying pan and cover with the lid. Cook until puffed bubbles appear
on the top surface.

If you are cooking on a gas flame, using long tongs, hold the uncooked
side over the flame to give an authentically charred result. Brush the
charred side with butter and sprinkle with nigella seeds. If you are
cooking on an electric stove, brush butter over the uncooked side and
sprinkle with nigella seeds. Flip and cook in the pan until browned.

Brush this surface with butter, sprinkle with nigella seeds and flip it
gently. Cook this side until slightly charred. Transfer the cooked naan
to a plate. Repeat with the remaining dough.

 ★ ★ ★

SPAGHETTI BOLOGNESE
FRITTATA

SERVES 4

1 TABLESPOON OLIVE OIL

1 LARGE RED ONION, FINELY CHOPPED

4 GARLIC CLOVES, MINCED

2 BAY LEAVES

¼ CUP (60ML) RED WINE

2 TABLESPOONS BALSAMIC VINEGAR

600G VEAL MINCE

400G CAN DICED TOMATOES

2 CUPS (600G) TOMATO PASSATA

¼ CUP CHOPPED FRESH BASIL LEAVES

1 TABLESPOON FRESH CHOPPED ROSEMARY

1 TEASPOON DRIED OREGANO

1 CUP (250ML) CHICKEN STOCK

250G SPAGHETTI

4 EGGS

BASIL LEAVES AND FRESHLY GRATED PARMESAN
CHEESE, TO SERVE

Heat the olive oil in a large heavy-bottomed saucepan on medium heat. Add the onion, garlic and bay leaves. Sauté for a few minutes until onion starts caramelising. Deglaze the pan with the red wine and balsamic vinegar.

Add the veal mince and break up the meat evenly using a wooden spoon as it cooks. Add tomatoes and passata. Mix well. Stir in the basil, rosemary, oregano and chicken stock.

Reduce the heat to low, cover and simmer for 30 minutes, stirring occasionally. Season with salt and freshly ground black pepper to taste.

Meanwhile, cook the spaghetti in a large saucepan of salted boiling water until al dente. Drain well.

Divide the spaghetti between two small cast-iron frying pans (20cm). Top with enough Bolognese sauce to cover the spaghetti. Crack two eggs over the sauce in each pan. Place under a hot grill and cook until eggs are set. Serve hot with basil leaves and lots of freshly grated parmesan cheese.

Leftover bolognese sauce will keep in the fridge for up to 3 days, or you can freeze it.

★ ★ ★

Everyone I know loves a good sweet and sour dish. Chinese restaurants often ruin it with too much sweetness and colour. This is a well-balanced sweet and sour dish made with roast potatoes. It definitely gives pork a run for its money!

SWEET & SOUR
POTATOES

SERVES 4

6 MEDIUM POTATOES (ABOUT 650G)

½ TEASPOON SALT

4 TABLESPOONS VEGETABLE OIL

½ CUP SLICED CARROT

½ CUP CHOPPED GREEN CAPSICUM

½ CUP CHOPPED ONION

1 TEASPOON FINELY CHOPPED GINGER

1 CUP (250ML) CHICKEN STOCK

⅓ CUP (80ML) KETCHUP (TOMATO SAUCE)

¼ CUP (60ML) VINEGAR

1 TABLESPOON SOY SAUCE

1 TABLESPOON RAW SUGAR

1½ TABLESPOONS CORNFLOUR

¼ CUP DICED PINEAPPLE

¼ TEASPOON WHITE OR BLACK PEPPER

¼ CUP SLICED SPRING ONIONS TO GARNISH (GREEN PART)

STEAMED RICE, TO SERVE

Preheat the oven to 200°C and line a baking tray with baking paper.

Scrub the potatoes and pat dry with paper towels. Cut into 2.5cm pieces. Combine in a bowl with the salt and half the oil. Toss to mix and coat. Spread out onto the prepared tray and bake for 30 minutes until golden and crunchy. Remove from the oven and set aside.

Heat the remaining vegetable oil in a saucepan on high heat. Add the carrot, capsicum, onion and ginger. Sauté for a minute, then reduce the heat to medium. Stir in the stock, ketchup, vinegar, soy sauce and sugar. Cook for a minute or two. Mix the cornflour with ¼ cup (60ml) water to make a smooth paste. Add to the saucepan with the pineapple and pepper. Mix well.

Add the potatoes to the pan, reduce the heat to low and simmer for a few minutes until the sauce thickens. Remove from heat, garnish with spring onions and serve hot with rice.

ROAST TANDOORI
CHICKEN

SERVES 4

This tandoori chicken paste is my secret recipe and I've always kept it close. It is the real deal and the gorgeous hue comes from beetroot and not artificial colour. A jar of this paste sits happily in the fridge for up to a week. Before long you will find yourself marinating fish, potatoes and even succulent little quails.

4 CHICKEN MARYLAND PIECES

1 TABLESPOON NATURAL YOGHURT

SPRAY COOKING OIL

LEMON WEDGES, SLICED ONION AND MINT YOGHURT, TO SERVE

TANDOORI PASTE

2 TABLESPOONS GROUND CUMIN

1 TABLESPOON GARAM MASALA

3 TEASPOONS SWEET PAPRIKA

1 TEASPOON GROUND CINNAMON

1 TEASPOON GROUND CARDAMOM

1 TEASPOON RED CHILLI FLAKES

½ TEASPOON GROUND NUTMEG

½ TEASPOON WHOLE BLACK PEPPERCORNS

2 BAY LEAVES

¼ CUP (60ML) VEGETABLE OIL

JUICE OF 1 LEMON

2 TABLESPOONS GARLIC PASTE

1 TABLESPOON GINGER PASTE

4 SLICES OF CANNED BEETROOT

HANDFUL OF FRESH CORIANDER LEAVES

1 TEASPOON SALT

To make the tandoori paste, combine all ingredients in a food processor and process until it forms a coarse paste.

Place the chicken pieces into a large bowl. Add the tandoori paste and yoghurt to the bowl. Using your fingers, massage the paste and yoghurt into the chicken, making sure it is well coated all over. Cover with cling wrap and marinate in the fridge for a couple of hours or overnight.

Preheat the oven to 200°C and line a baking tray with foil. Heat a chargrill pan on high heat. Spray the chicken liberally with oil and cook on the chargrill, turning once, until nicely charred.

Transfer to the tray, and roast for 20–30 minutes, until cooked through (pierce the thickest part with a skewer – juices will run clear when cooked). Set aside to rest for a few minutes. Serve with lemon wedges, sliced onion and mint yoghurt.

If you don't have a chargrill pan, brown the chicken under a grill for about 8 minutes each side, before finishing in the oven as directed.

CRUNCHY HARISSA ROASTED POTATOES
WITH COOL YOGHURT DIP

SERVES 4

Fiery harissa paste is the key to the success of these delightfully crunchy and spicy potatoes. You will find it at speciality grocers or delicatessens.

650G KIPFLER POTATOES

FINELY GRATED ZEST OF 1 LEMON

1 TABLESPOON HARISSA PASTE

1 TEASPOON GARLIC GRANULES

1 TABLESPOON PLAIN FLOUR

YOGHURT DIP

1 CUP (280G) GREEK YOGHURT

1 SMALL CUCUMBER, GRATED

HANDFUL OF MINT LEAVES, FINELY CHOPPED

HANDFUL OF CORIANDER LEAVES, FINELY CHOPPED

1 TEASPOON CASTER SUGAR

To make the dip, mix all the ingredients in a bowl and season with salt and freshly ground black pepper, to taste. Set aside.

Preheat the oven to 220°C and line a baking tray with baking paper. Scrub the potatoes and pat dry with paper towels. Cut each potato crossways into four thick slices. Place into a saucepan of salted water and bring to the boil. Cook for 10 minutes, then drain well.

Place the potatoes into a large bowl. Add the lemon zest, harissa paste, garlic and flour. Season with salt, and mix until evenly coated.

Spread the potatoes onto the prepared tray and bake for 12 minutes, or until lightly golden brown. Serve with yoghurt dip.

★ ★ ★

FEAST OF MUSHROOMS
WITH PEANUT BUTTER MISO GLAZE

SERVES 2

550G MIXED MUSHROOMS (BUTTON, BROWN, PORTOBELLO, SHIMEJI)

3 TABLESPOONS SESAME OIL

2 GARLIC CLOVES, CHOPPED

2 TABLESPOONS SOY SAUCE

2 TABLESPOONS WHITE WINE

4 TABLESPOONS PEANUT BUTTER MISO GLAZE (SEE OPPOSITE)

SNOW PEA SPROUTS, SLIVERED NORI, SESAME SEEDS AND SLICED SPRING ONIONS, TO SERVE

PEANUT BUTTER MISO GLAZE (MAKES 1½ CUPS)

¼ CUP (60ML) RICE WINE VINEGAR

¼ CUP (60ML) PEANUT OIL

3 TABLESPOONS TAHINI

2 TABLESPOONS PEANUT BUTTER

2 TABLESPOONS RED MISO PASTE

1 TABLESPOON SESAME OIL

1 TABLESPOON BROWN SUGAR

1 GARLIC CLOVE

2.5CM PIECE GINGER, PEELED

To make the peanut butter miso glaze, place all the ingredients into a food processor with ¼ cup (60ml) water, and process until a smooth paste forms. Season with salt and freshly ground black pepper to taste. Store in a lidded glass jar in the fridge for up to a week.

Slice the mushrooms as desired. Heat the oil in a large sauté pan on high heat. Add the garlic and sauté for a few seconds. Add the mushrooms and toss to coat in the oil. Add the soy sauce and white wine. Cook, tossing constantly, until the wine evaporates.

Add the peanut butter miso glaze and mix well. Cook for a minute, until the glaze has heated through. Serve immediately, topped with sprouts, nori, sesame seeds and spring onions.

★ ★ ★

WHOLEMEAL PASTA
WITH GARLIC CRUMBS

SERVES 4

300G WHOLEMEAL SPAGHETTI

60G BUTTER

2 TABLESPOONS OLIVE OIL

8 GARLIC CLOVES, CHOPPED

10 SAGE LEAVES, FINELY CHOPPED

½ CUP (20G) FRESH BREADCRUMBS

½ CUP (90G) RAW ALMONDS, CRUSHED

JUICE OF 1 LEMON

HANDFUL OF CHERRY TOMATOES, HALVED

1 CUP FINELY CHOPPED SPINACH

½ CUP CHOPPED BASIL

¼ CUP (20G) FINELY GRATED ROMANO CHEESE,
PLUS EXTRA TO SERVE

Cook the spaghetti in a large saucepan of salted boiling water until al dente. Drain well.

Heat the butter and oil in a heavy-bottomed frying pan on medium heat. Add the garlic and sauté until crispy. Add the sage, breadcrumbs, almonds and lemon juice. Sauté for a few minutes on low heat until fragrant. Add the tomatoes, spinach and basil. Cook for a minute or two until the spinach has wilted.

Add the spaghetti to the pan and toss to mix well. Cook for 1–2 minutes or until heated through. Remove from heat, add cheese and season with salt and freshly ground black pepper. Mix well. Serve with extra cheese.

★ ★ ★

This curry owes its creaminess to cashew nuts. It is totally moreish and will have you dipping in with a spoon. I've cooked it here with pea, spinach and tofu, but you could make it your own with sliced green beans, paneer, carrot, snow peas, chicken or even prawns.

CREAMY PEA & SPINACH
CURRY WITH TOFU

SERVES 4

¾ CUP (115G) CASHEW NUTS	1 TEASPOON SUGAR
2 RED ONIONS, ROUGHLY CHOPPED	2 TEASPOONS GROUND CUMIN
½ TEASPOON GINGER PASTE	1 TEASPOON GROUND CORIANDER
4–5 BLACK PEPPERCORNS	¼ TEASPOON GROUND CARDAMOM
1 TABLESPOON BUTTER	300G FIRM TOFU, CUBED
1 BAY LEAF	1 CUP FINELY CHOPPED SPINACH
1½ TEASPOONS SALT	1½ CUP PEAS (FROZEN OR FRESH)

Place the cashew nuts in a heatproof bowl and cover with 1 cup (250ml) boiling water. Leave to soak for 10 minutes, then drain.

Place the cashews nuts, onion, ginger paste, peppercorns and 2 cups (500ml) water into a blender and process until smooth.

Heat the butter in a heavy-bottomed saucepan on medium-low heat. Add the cashew nut mixture, bay leaf, salt, sugar, cumin, coriander and cardamom. Mix well. Cook for about 10 minutes, stirring occasionally, until the sauce appears toasted and a shade darker.

Add the tofu, spinach and peas. Reduce the heat to low and simmer for 15–20 minutes until reduced and thickened slightly.

★ ★ ★

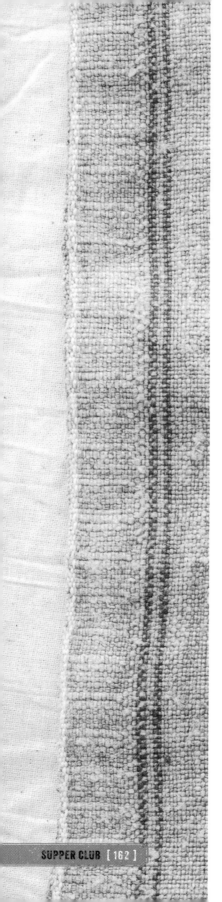

NICK'S MINCED LAMB TACOS
WITH LENTIL & CORN RELISH

SERVES 4

1 TABLESPOON OLIVE OIL

3 BAY LEAVES

1 SMALL RED ONION, FINELY CHOPPED

500G LAMB MINCE

1 CUP (150G) FROZEN PEAS

3 TEASPOONS GROUND CUMIN

1 TEASPOON SMOKED PAPRIKA

½ TEASPOON GROUND CINNAMON

8 WHOLEMEAL TORTILLAS, WARMED

HOT CHILLI SAUCE, TO SERVE

LEMON WEDGES, TO SERVE

LENTIL & CORN RELISH

1 CUP (140G) CORN KERNELS

1 CUP CANNED LENTILS, RINSED AND DRAINED

1 MEDIUM TOMATO, FINELY CHOPPED

HANDFUL OF CORIANDER LEAVES, CHOPPED

JUICE OF 1 LEMON

To make the relish, mix all the ingredients in a medium bowl. Season with salt and freshly ground black pepper, and toss to combine. Cover and set aside.

Heat the oil in a heavy-bottomed saucepan. Add the bay leaves and cook for a few seconds, until fragrant. Add the onion and sauté on low heat until soft and golden. Add the lamb mince and break it up nicely using a wooden spoon, tossing and stirring as it cooks, until browned. Add frozen peas, cumin, paprika and cinnamon. Season with salt and mix well.

Cover and simmer on low heat for about 40 minutes, stirring occasionally. Remove from heat and set aside.

To assemble tacos, spoon the lamb mixture onto tortillas, and top with relish and hot chilli sauce. Serve with lemon wedges.

★ ★ ★

FETA, ROAST GARLIC
& **BEETROOT DIP**

MAKES 1 1/2 CUPS

8 GARLIC CLOVES, UNPEELED

450G CAN WHOLE BABY BEETROOT, DRAINED

1/4 TEASPOON SALT

FEW SPRIGS OF FRESH THYME, LEAVES PICKED

50G FETA CHEESE, PLUS EXTRA FOR TOP

1 TABLESPOON OLIVE OIL, PLUS EXTRA FOR TOP

1 TEASPOON RAW SUGAR

1 TEASPOON BALSAMIC VINEGAR

Preheat the oven to 200°C. Place the garlic cloves onto a baking tray and bake for 30 minutes. Cool slightly.

Place the remaining ingredients into a food processor, and add the roasted garlic, squeezed from the skins. Process to a coarse paste. Transfer to a bowl. Crumble the extra feta over and drizzle with oil.

★ ★ ★

MASALA **CLAMS**

700G CLAMS

1 TABLESPOON OLIVE OIL

1 TABLESPOON BUTTER

8-10 CASHEW NUTS, CRUSHED

4 GARLIC CLOVES, MINCED

1 RED ONION, FINELY CHOPPED

1 TEASPOON GARAM MASALA

½ TEASPOON GROUND TURMERIC

1 CUP (250ML) WHITE WINE

HANDFUL OF FRESH CORIANDER LEAVES

LEMON WEDGES AND TOASTED BREAD, TO SERVE

Place the clams into a large bowl of cold salted water for half an hour (this will make the clams spit the sand out). Lift the clams out and place into another bowl.

Heat the oil and butter in a large saucepan on medium heat. Sauté the cashew nuts, garlic and onion for a few minutes until they start browning. Add the garam masala, turmeric, wine and ½ cup (125ml) water.

Reduce the heat to low. Add the clams, cover with a lid and steam for 25–30 minutes until the clams have opened. Remove from the heat and discard any clams that haven't opened. Season with salt.

Garnish with coriander leaves. Serve with lemon wedges and toasted bread.

★ ★ ★

STICKY CARAMEL
CHICKEN WINGS

SERVES 6

1KG CHICKEN WINGS

2 TABLESPOONS GARLIC PASTE

1 TABLESPOON KECAP MANIS (SWEET SOY SAUCE)

1 TABLESPOON OLIVE OIL

1½ TEASPOONS SALT

½ TEASPOON GROUND CHILLI

CHOPPED CHIVES, TO SERVE

STICKY CARAMEL SAUCE

½ CUP (100G) BROWN SUGAR

2 TABLESPOONS FISH SAUCE

2 TABLESPOONS LEMON JUICE

1 TEASPOON LIGHT SOY SAUCE

Place the chicken wings into a large bowl. Add the garlic paste, kecap manis, oil, salt and ground chilli. Mix well. Cover with cling wrap and refrigerate for an hour.

To make the sauce, heat a small heavy-bottomed saucepan on medium heat. Add the brown sugar and stir for a few seconds until it starts melting and caramelising. Reduce the heat to low and add the fish sauce, lemon juice and light soy sauce. Add ¼ cup (60ml) water and bring to a simmer. Cook for about 10 minutes, or until the sauce becomes sticky and thickens slightly. Remove from the heat and cool completely.

Preheat the oven to 200°C. Place the marinated chicken onto a large baking tray. Bake for 30–40 minutes, turning the chicken once halfway through cooking, until it is browned and starting to crisp. Serve hot with sticky caramel sauce and chives.

★ ★ ★

WHOLEMEAL
PIZZA DOUGH

MAKES 4 LARGE
FAMILY-SIZED PIZZAS

2 TEASPOONS DRY YEAST

2 TEASPOONS SUGAR

2 TABLESPOONS OLIVE OIL

350G STRONG BREAD FLOUR

200G WHOLEMEAL PLAIN FLOUR

50G SEMOLINA

1½ TEASPOONS SALT

EXTRA BREAD FLOUR, FOR DUSTING

SPRAY COOKING OIL FOR BOWL

Place 350ml warm water into a bowl and add the yeast, sugar and olive oil. Mix gently and set aside for 10 minutes until the mixture is frothy.

Combine the bread flour, wholemeal flour, semolina and salt in a large bowl. Make a well in the centre, and pour the yeast mixture into the well. Using a wooden spoon, mix the dough gently until it comes together.

Dust a clean work surface with bread flour. Place the barely mixed dough onto the floured surface. Using your hands, knead the dough, pushing forward with the heel of your palm and bringing it towards you with the fingers in a repeating motion. Knead for a few minutes until a smooth dough is formed. Use a tiny bit of flour to dust if you feel the dough is too sticky and unmanageable.

Spray the inside of a clean bowl with cooking oil, and place the kneaded dough into the bowl. Cover with a clean tea towel and place in a warm area of your kitchen for 1–2 hours. At the end of this rising stage, your pizza dough will have doubled in size. It is now ready to use.

SYDNEY **PIZZA**

MAKES 4 LARGE PIZZAS

*Our first meal in Sydney was a pizza called Kathmandu. It had,
as the name suggests, Nepalese flavours. That night we talked
about what a Sydney pizza would taste like. After several years
of exploring the local food scene, this pizza is my ode to this
remarkable city's sun, surf, sea and turf!*

1 QUANTITY PIZZA DOUGH (SEE PAGE 171)

400G BOTTLE NAPOLETANA SAUCE

½ CUP (125ML) BARBECUE SAUCE

1 TEASPOON DRIED OREGANO

350G CHICKEN THIGH FILLETS

1 TABLESPOON MELTED BUTTER

FEW SPRIGS OF THYME, LEAVES PICKED

1 TEASPOON GARLIC PASTE

300G FRESH TIGER PRAWNS, PEELED AND
DEVEINED, TAILS ON

3 TABLESPOONS SWEET CHILLI SAUCE

1 SMALL HEAD OF BROCCOLI, SEPARATED
INTO FLORETS

10 SNOW PEAS, HALVED LENGTHWISE

RED CHILLI FLAKES (TO YOUR TASTE)

1 CUP (100G) MOZZARELLA CHEESE, SHREDDED

OLIVE OIL, TO DRIZZLE

Preheat the oven to 220°C. Divide the dough into four equal
balls. Using floured fingers, gently stretch each dough ball
thinly to a desired shape (it doesn't have to be round!), about
5mm thick. Place the dough onto a pizza stone or baking tray
lined with baking paper.

Combine the Napoletana sauce, barbecue sauce and oregano
in a bowl. Combine the chicken, melted butter, thyme and
garlic paste in another bowl, and season with salt. Toss the
prawns and sweet chilli sauce together in another bowl.

Spread a quarter of the sauce onto each pizza base. Top with
a quarter of the chicken mixture, prawns, broccoli, snow peas,
chilli flakes and mozzarella cheese. Drizzle with olive oil. Bake
for 12–15 minutes, until crispy and cooked through. Cut into
wedges and serve hot. Repeat with the remaining ingredients
to make four pizzas.

★ ★ ★

I am often asked what is my signature dish. It's a question you cannot escape as a food blogger. My answer is always the same – chicken curry! I learned to cook it from my dad, and the recipe has evolved over the years. Out of the dozen or so variations that I cook, this one is truly wonderful with the addition of cauliflower and chickpeas. Once I successfully made it at camp on a little flame burner, which should tell you how easy and versatile it is!

CHICKEN CURRY
WITH CAULIFLOWER & CHICKPEAS

SERVES 10

2 TABLESPOONS GHEE OR BUTTER

12 GARLIC CLOVES, MINCED

1 TABLESPOON GINGER PASTE

3 BAY LEAVES

1 CINNAMON STICK

4 CLOVES

2 LARGE RED ONIONS, FINELY CHOPPED

1 LARGE RED CHILLI, SLICED

1 CUP FINELY CHOPPED CORIANDER LEAVES & STALKS

1KG CHICKEN DRUMSTICKS

2 TABLESPOONS GROUND CUMIN

1 TEASPOON GROUND TURMERIC

1 TEASPOON GROUND CARDAMOM

1 TEASPOON GARAM MASALA

A DASH OF NUTMEG

A DASH OF FRESHLY GROUND BLACK PEPPER

2 TEASPOONS SALT

600G TOMATO PASSATA

410G CAN CHICKPEAS, RINSED AND DRAINED

2 CUPS CAULIFLOWER FLORETS

HANDFUL OF CORIANDER LEAVES

NAAN, TO SERVE

Melt the ghee or butter in a large (5-litre capacity) flameproof casserole or heavy-bottomed saucepan on high heat. Add the garlic, ginger paste, bay leaves, cinnamon and cloves. Sauté for a few seconds until fragrant. Reduce the heat to medium and add the onion, chilli, coriander leaves and stalks and chicken. Cook for a few minutes until the chicken starts to brown and the onion is soft.

Add all the spices, salt, passata, chickpeas and 1 cup (250ml) water. Cover and simmer for 30 minutes on low. Give it a stir, add the cauliflower, cover and simmer for another 30 minutes until piping hot and the cauliflower is tender. Serve garnished with coriander leaves, and naan on the side.

★ ★ ★

THIRSTIES

1. COLD-PRESSED ICED COFFEE

COFFEE CONCENTRATE (SERVES 8)

200G GROUND COFFEE
4 CUPS (1 LITRE) COLD WATER

ICED COFFEE (MAKES 1)

1 CUP ICE CUBES
¼ CUP (60ML) COFFEE CONCENTRATE
GENEROUS DRIZZLE OF CONDENSED MILK
MILK, TO SERVE

To make the coffee concentrate, place the ground coffee and cold water into a large jug. Mix well. Allow to steep for 6 hours or overnight. Using a nut milk bag or a combination of a sieve and muslin cloth, allow the coffee mix to strain over an hour without pressing down on the solids. Discard the coffee dregs. Pour the strained coffee into a bottle and store in the fridge for up to 2 weeks.

To make the iced coffee, place the ice cubes into a 500ml glass jar or tall glass. Pour the coffee concentrate over the ice. Top up with condensed milk and milk to your taste. Mix well and serve.

GREEN MANGO COOLER

- 2 GREEN MANGOES
- JUICE OF 2 LEMONS
- ¾ CUP (165G) RAW SUGAR
- ¼ TEASPOON SALT
- CHILLED SPARKLING WATER, TO TASTE
- MINT SPRIGS, TO SERVE

Peel the mangoes and cut the flesh into little pieces. Place into a small heavy-bottomed saucepan with the lemon juice, sugar and salt. Cook on low heat for about 30 minutes, stirring occasionally, until the mixture reaches a jam consistency. Add ½ cup (125ml) water and cook for another 5 minutes. Remove from the heat and cool completely. Store in a jar in the fridge for up to a week.

To serve, spoon 2–3 tablespoons of mango jam into a tall glass. Top with chilled sparkling water and serve with fresh mint sprigs.

★ ★ ★

3. ICED LEMON TEA

- 6 TEASPOONS OF STRONG TEA LEAVES (MORNING BREAKFAST OR ASSAM TEA)
- 6 CUPS (1.5 LITRES) BOILING WATER
- 3 CUPS (750ML) CHILLED WATER
- JUICE OF 6 LEMONS
- ¼ CUP (55G) CASTER SUGAR
- ¼ TEASPOON SALT
- 1 LEMON, THINLY SLICED
- HANDFUL OF FRESH MINT LEAVES
- 1 CUP ICE CUBES

Brew tea using the tea leaves and boiling water. Allow to steep for 4–6 minutes for a strong brew. Strain the tea and discard the tea leaves. Cool completely.

In a large jug, mix the chilled water with the lemon juice, sugar and salt. Set aside, stirring occasionally, until the sugar has dissolved. Pour the strained tea into the jug. Top with lemon slices, mint sprigs and ice cubes. Serve.

★ ★ ★

TREAT FACTORY

A naughty little something is the perfect way to end
a special meal. These delectable desserts are intriguing enough to
keep everyone coming back for seconds. Satisfy your sweet tooth
with no-bake treats, low-sugar cakes oozing with flavour, creamy
ice-creams, sensational yoghurts, cheeky brownies
and even a healthy chocolate cake!

AND

NAUGHTIES

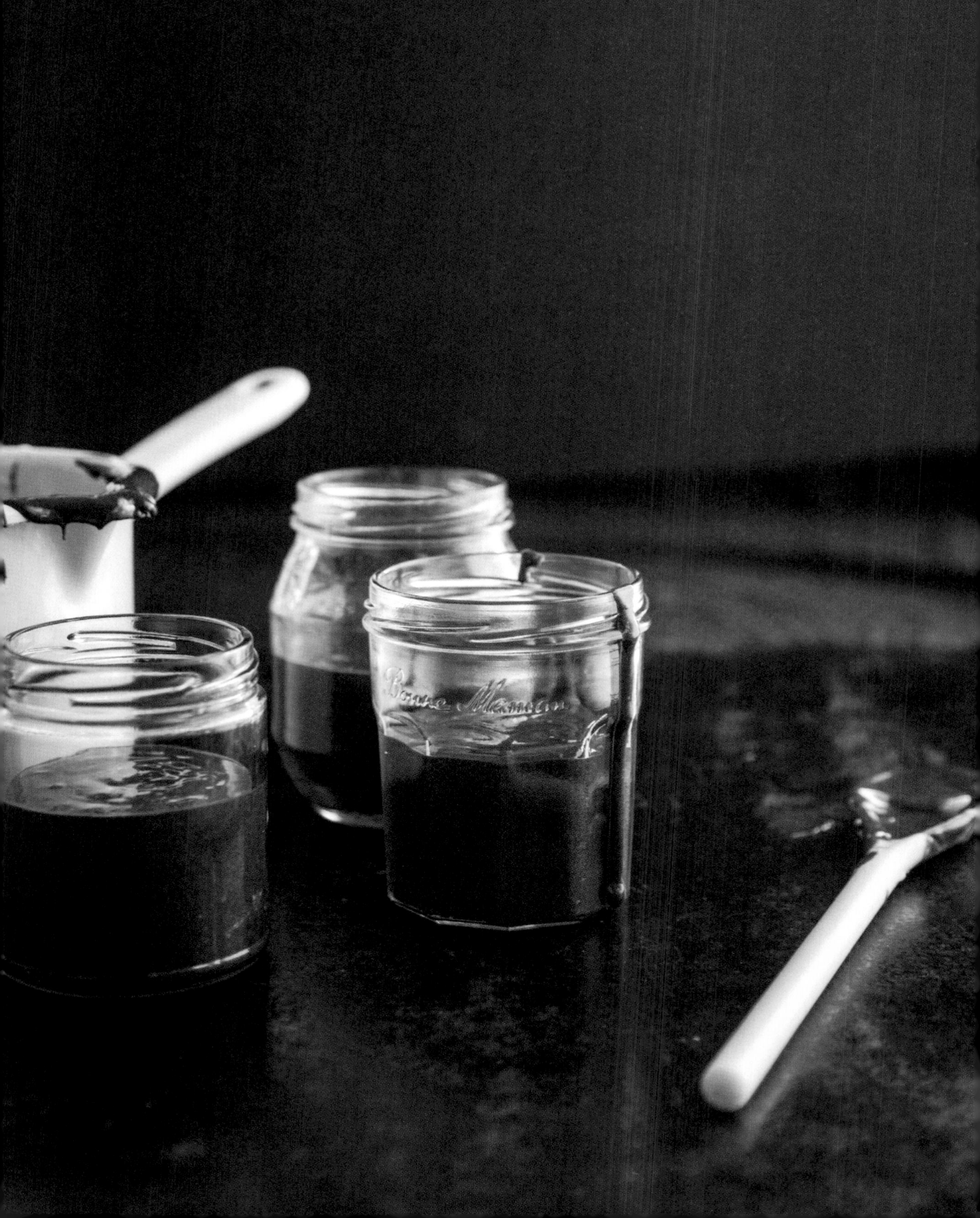
Bonne Maman

This is a fun variation on the traditional clafoutis: a French dessert of cherries baked into a sweet and silky flan. My version uses dollops of Nutella instead of cherries, which instantly makes it more indulgent and magical!

NUTELLA
CLAFOUTIS

SERVES 6

BUTTER, FOR GREASING

RAW SUGAR, FOR SPRINKLING

1 CUP (250G) NUTELLA (OR ANY HAZELNUT SPREAD)

1/3 CUP (50G) PLAIN FLOUR

1/2 CUP (110G) CASTER SUGAR

1/2 CUP (125ML) MILK

3/4 CUP (185ML) CREAM

1 TEASPOON VANILLA EXTRACT

4 EGGS

CREAM AND TOASTED HAZELNUTS, TO SERVE

Preheat the oven to 180°C. Grease a 6 cup shallow ovenproof dish with butter and sprinkle with raw sugar. Scoop Nutella with a melon baller or teaspoon and drop the dollops into the dish.

Mix the flour, sugar and milk in a bowl with an electric mixer. Add cream, vanilla and eggs and whisk until smooth.

Pour the mixture into the dish over the Nutella. Bake for about 35 minutes until puffed-up and golden. Serve warm with cream and toasted hazelnuts.

★ ★ ★

BOOZY CHOCOLATE
NUTELLA POTS

SERVES 4-6

200G DARK CHOCOLATE, BROKEN INTO BIG PIECES

50G BUTTER, CHOPPED

⅓ CUP (80G) NUTELLA

EGGS, SEPARATED

⅓ CUP (75G) CASTER SUGAR

50ML PURE CREAM

50ML POURING CREAM

TABLESPOONS ICING SUGAR

TABLESPOONS IRISH CREAM LIQUEUR (OR RUM
OR TIA MARIA OR KAHLUA)

Combine the chocolate, butter, Nutella and ⅓ cup
(80ml) water in a heavy-bottomed saucepan on low
heat. Cook the mixture for a few minutes, stirring
constantly, until melted and glossy. Remove from
the heat and cool.

Place the egg yolks and caster sugar into a separate
bowl and whisk until pale and creamy.

Add egg yolk mixture to chocolate mixture and mix
with a wooden spoon until thoroughly mixed, thick
and glossy.

Place the eggwhites into a clean bowl and beat with
electric beaters until stiff peaks form.

Fold the eggwhites into the chocolate mixture until
evenly combined.

Pour the mixture into glasses or jars. Cover and
refrigerate for 2–3 hours until set.

Just before serving, whisk the pure cream, pouring
cream, icing sugar and liqueur in a bowl until thick
(like buttercream icing). Spoon into the chocolate
pots, and serve.

★ ★ ★

This recipe came about by chance when I was baking a traditional chocolate caramel slice and over-baked the caramel layer. Hooray for happy accidents!

BURNT BUTTER
CARAMEL SLICE

SERVES 8-10

COOKIE BASE

1 CUP (150G) PLAIN FLOUR

½ CUP (45G) DESICCATED COCONUT

½ CUP (100G) BROWN SUGAR

125G BUTTER, MELTED

BURNT BUTTER CARAMEL TOPPING

395G CAN SWEETENED CONDENSED MILK

125G BUTTER, MELTED

⅓ CUP (80ML) GOLDEN SYRUP

Preheat oven to 180°C. Grease a 20cm x 30cm slice tin and line with baking paper, hanging over the two long sides. To make the cookie base, place flour, coconut, sugar and butter into a bowl and mix well. Press the mixture into the base of the prepared tin. Bake for 15 minutes until golden.

For the topping, place the condensed milk, butter and golden syrup into a saucepan over low heat. Cook for 5–7 minutes, stirring constantly to avoid sticking, until the caramel has thickened and is smooth.

Pour the caramel mixture onto the cookie layer. Bake for 20 to 25 minutes, until the caramel is golden and starts browning in spots (the burnt butter effect!).

Set aside to cool for 20 minutes, slice and serve warm.

★ ★ ★

FERRERO ROCHER
BROWNIES

SERVES 12

Brownie lovers, hold on to your hats. There is a chocolate truffle in each slice! These are the creamiest surprise brownies I have ever had the pleasure of baking.

300G GOOD-QUALITY DARK CHOCOLATE, BROKEN UP

100G UNSALTED BUTTER, CHOPPED

200G CASTER SUGAR

½ CUP (75G) PLAIN FLOUR

⅓ CUP (30G) COCOA POWDER, PLUS EXTRA TO DUST

2 TEASPOONS BAKING POWDER

¼ TEASPOON SALT

4 EGGS

½ CUP (120G) SOUR CREAM

75G PITTED PRUNES, CHOPPED

12 FERRERO ROCHER CHOCOLATES

Preheat the oven to 170°C. Grease a 20cm x 30cm slice tin and line with baking paper, hanging over the two long sides.

Put the chocolate, butter and sugar into a heatproof bowl and sit over a pan of barely simmering water, making sure the base of the bowl does not touch the water. Stir for 10 minutes until the chocolate has melted. Stir to combine and allow to cool.

Sift the flour, cocoa, baking powder and salt into a bowl. Add the eggs one at a time to the chocolate mixture and mix with electric beaters until well combined. Add the dry ingredients and sour cream and mix with the beaters. Stir in the prunes gently until just combined.

Arrange the Ferrero Rocher chocolates in the prepared tin, in 3 rows of four. Spoon the mixture over the chocolates carefully, making sure not to move them. Bake for 1 hour, until just set. Allow to cool completely in the tin before lifting out.

Dip a knife in hot water, dry, and cut to make neat squares. Dust with cocoa powder. The brownies will keep for up to 3 days in an airtight container in a cool spot of your kitchen.

★ ★ ★

TRIPLE CHOCOLATE
FRIANDS

SERVES 9

BUTTER, FOR GREASING

DRY BREADCRUMBS, FOR DUSTING

150G BUTTER

5 EGGWHITES

¼ CUP (40G) PLAIN FLOUR

2 TABLESPOONS DARK COCOA POWDER

¼ TEASPOON BAKING POWDER

PINCH OF SALT

1 CUP (120G) HAZELNUT MEAL

¾ CUP (165G) CASTER SUGAR

½ CUP (90G) MILK CHOCOLATE BITS

¼ CUP (45G) WHITE CHOCOLATE BITS

ICING SUGAR, TO DUST

Preheat the oven to 180°C. Grease 9 holes of a
12-hole friand tin with butter. Dust with breadcrumbs
and shake excess off.

Melt the butter in a heavy-bottomed saucepan on
low heat. Simmer until bubbling and a shade darker.
Remove from the heat and set aside.

Place the eggwhites in a clean dry bowl. Whisk until
frothy and voluminous.

Sift the flour, cocoa powder, baking powder and salt
in a large bowl. Add the hazelnut meal, sugar and
milk chocolate bits. Mix gently. Add the eggwhites
and butter. Using a wooden spoon, mix the batter
until well combined and smooth.

Spoon the batter into the prepared tin. Top with white
chocolate bits and bake for about 15 minutes, or until
firm to a gentle touch in the centre. Cool in the tin
slightly before gently prising the friands out with a butter
knife while still warm. Serve with a dusting of icing sugar.

★ ★ ★

My boys do not eat a cake with icing except when it is their own birthday and I am about to throw a fit because they won't eat their birthday cake. To be honest, I prefer plain cakes too. So I try to bake my cakes light and loaded with irresistible tastes. This lemon cake is a perfect example: sour, sweet, tangy and summery, all presented in a bright canary package.

LEMON CAKE

SERVES 8

125G BUTTER, SOFTENED

1 CUP (220G) CASTER SUGAR

FINELY GRATED ZEST OF 2 LARGE LEMONS

3 EGGS

1½ CUPS (225G) SELF-RAISING FLOUR

JUICE OF 1 LARGE LEMON

½ CUP (125ML) MILK

Preheat the oven to 180°C. Grease a 20cm cake tin and line the base with baking paper.

Using electric beaters, beat the butter, sugar and zest in a bowl until creamy and fluffy. Add the eggs one at a time, beating after each addition. Sift the flour over the egg mixture. Add juice and beat for a few seconds. Add the milk and beat until just combined.

Pour into the prepared tin. Tap the tin gently on the worktop to settle the batter. Bake for 45–50 minutes until golden and cooked through when tested with a skewer.

Stand cake in the tin for 5 minutes, then turn onto a wire rack to cool slightly.

Serve warm just by itself, or cool and dust with icing sugar.

When I have a couple of fresh, unsprayed roses blooming in the garden, I chop up the petals and bake them into this cake. Their fragrant taste is delicately exotic. When I don't have roses on hand, I use rosewater, as in this recipe. This is a true celebration cake, minus the sugary icing. It is pretty as a picture too!

ROSE & PISTACHIO CAKE
WITH FRESH RASPBERRIES

SERVES 8–10

125G BUTTER, SOFTENED

1 CUP (220G) CASTER SUGAR

1 TABLESPOON FINELY GRATED ORANGE ZEST

1 TABLESPOON ROSEWATER

2 EGGS

2 CUPS (300G) PLAIN FLOUR

2½ TEASPOONS BAKING POWDER

¼ TEASPOON SALT

⅔ CUP (165ML) MILK

¼ CUP (70G) GREEK YOGHURT

½ CUP (60G) FROZEN RASPBERRIES

½ CUP (65G) PISTACHIO KERNELS, CHOPPED

ICING SUGAR, TO DUST

FRESH RASPBERRIES AND CREAM, TO SERVE

Preheat the oven to 180°C. Grease a 20cm round cake tin and line the base with baking paper.

Place the butter, sugar, orange zest and rosewater into the bowl of an electric mixer and beat for 6 minutes on low until light and creamy. Add the eggs and beat well.

Sift the flour, baking powder and salt into a bowl, and add the butter mixture, and the milk and yoghurt. Fold together until just combined. Gently fold through the frozen raspberries and pistachios.

Spoon the mixture into the prepared tin and bake for 50–55 minutes, until golden and cooked through when tested with a skewer.
Cool in the tin for 5 minutes, then turn out onto a wire rack and cool completely.

Dust with icing sugar, and serve with fresh raspberries and cream.

★ ★ ★

This cake has farmhouse written all over it. It is rustic, dark, crumbly and full of crunch. The aroma of the spices as it bakes will evoke visions of snowflakes and a warm crackling fire. I promise!

NUT CRUMBLE
& RYE CAKE

SERVES 8

125G BUTTER

½ CUP (110G) RAW SUGAR

2 EGGS

½ TEASPOON SALT

1 TEASPOON VANILLA EXTRACT

1 CUP (125G) RYE FLOUR

½ CUP (80G) PLAIN WHOLEMEAL FLOUR

½ CUP (60G) ALMOND MEAL

2 TEASPOONS BAKING POWDER

1 TEASPOON GROUND CARDAMOM

1 CUP (250ML) MILK

ICING SUGAR, TO DUST

CRUMBLE MIXTURE

60G BUTTER, MELTED

½ CUP (100G) BROWN SUGAR

2 TABLESPOONS PLAIN FLOUR

⅓ CUP FINELY CHOPPED PECAN NUTS

⅓ CUP FINELY CHOPPED ALMONDS

1 TEASPOON GROUND CINNAMON

1 TEASPOON GROUND CARDAMOM

Preheat the oven to 180°C. Grease a 20cm springform tin and line the base with baking paper.

Use electric beaters to beat the butter and sugar until creamy and pale. Add the eggs one at a time, beating after each addition. Add the salt and vanilla extract, and beat until fluffy.

Add the flours, almond meal, baking powder and cardamom. Add milk and beat until well combined. Spoon half the cake batter into the prepared tin.

Combine all ingredients for crumble mixture in a bowl and mix well. Sprinkle half the crumble mixture over the cake batter. Spoon the remaining cake batter into the tin. Top with the remaining crumble mixture. Bake for 40 minutes, or until firm to a gentle touch in the centre.

Cool in the tin slightly before releasing the sides and sliding onto a wire rack to cool. Lightly dust with icing sugar to serve.

★ ★ ★

Everyone should have a good chocolate cake recipe in their baking arsenal. This is a healthy version, if there is such a thing. It is light, moist, fudgy, utterly indulgent and baked with the goodness of nut oil and buttermilk. It becomes a real showstopper topped with seasonal red fruit and a dusting of powdered sugar.

CHOCOLATE
FUDGE CAKE

SERVES 8

¾ CUP (115G) PLAIN FLOUR

½ TEASPOON BAKING POWDER

5 TABLESPOONS DARK COCOA POWDER

1 CUP (200G) BROWN SUGAR

PINCH OF SALT

3 EGGS

¾ CUP (185ML) BUTTERMILK

⅓ CUP (80ML) MACADAMIA OIL
(OR RICE BRAN OIL OR VERY LIGHT OLIVE OIL)

1 TABLESPOON VANILLA EXTRACT

FRESH FIGS AND RED GRAPES, OR FRESH FRUIT IN SEASON

ICING SUGAR, FOR DUSTING

Preheat the oven to 160°C. Grease a 20cm round cake tin and line the base with baking paper.

Sift the flour, baking powder and cocoa powder into a large bowl. Add the sugar and salt, and stir to combine.

In a separate bowl, use electric beaters to beat the eggs, buttermilk, oil and vanilla extract until smooth. Add to the dry ingredients and beat for about a minute, until smooth.

Pour the cake mixture into the prepared tin and bake 35–40 minutes until just firm to a gentle touch in the centre. Remove from oven.

Cool cake completely in the tin. Turn out, invert onto a plate and decorate with fruit. Dust with icing sugar before serving.

★ ★ ★

This is one of my go-to desserts for Christmas. It smells divine! The addition of gingernut biscuits makes it more festive – ideal for the busy holiday season.

GINGERBREAD
TIRAMISU

SERVES 12

500G MASCARPONE

300ML POURING CREAM

1 CUP (250ML) STRONG ESPRESSO COFFEE (SEE NOTE)

1 CUP MARSALA OR ANY STRONG, SWEET LIQUEUR

500G SPONGE FINGERS (ITALIAN SAVOIARDI BISCUITS)

200G GINGERNUT (OR GINGERBREAD) BISCUITS, CRUSHED

GOOD-QUALITY COCOA POWDER, FOR DUSTING

Line a 20cm x 28cm (6cm deep) serving dish with baking paper, hanging over the two long sides. Use electric beaters to beat the mascarpone and pouring cream in a large bowl for a few minutes, until fluffy and light.

Combine the coffee and marsala in a large shallow dish. Working one at a time, dip sponge fingers briefly into the coffee mixture and lay them to cover the entire base of the prepared dish.

Spread one-third of the cream mixture on top in a smooth layer, and sprinkle with half the crushed gingernut biscuits.

Dip half of the remaining sponge fingers in the coffee mixture and make another layer on top of the cream mixture. Top with half the remaining cream mixture, and sprinkle with remaining gingernut biscuits. Dip the remaining sponge fingers in the coffee mixture and lay them over the crushed biscuits. Top with the remaining cream mixture. Smooth the surface, and dust generously with cocoa powder.

Cover with cling wrap and chill in the fridge for at least 2 hours before serving. Use the overhanging paper to lift out of the dish, and cut into portions to serve.

★ ★ ★

I made the coffee in a plunger, 3–4 scoops of coffee in about 1 cup (250ml) hot water. Alternatively, mix 3–4 teaspoons instant coffee in 1 cup (250ml) hot water.

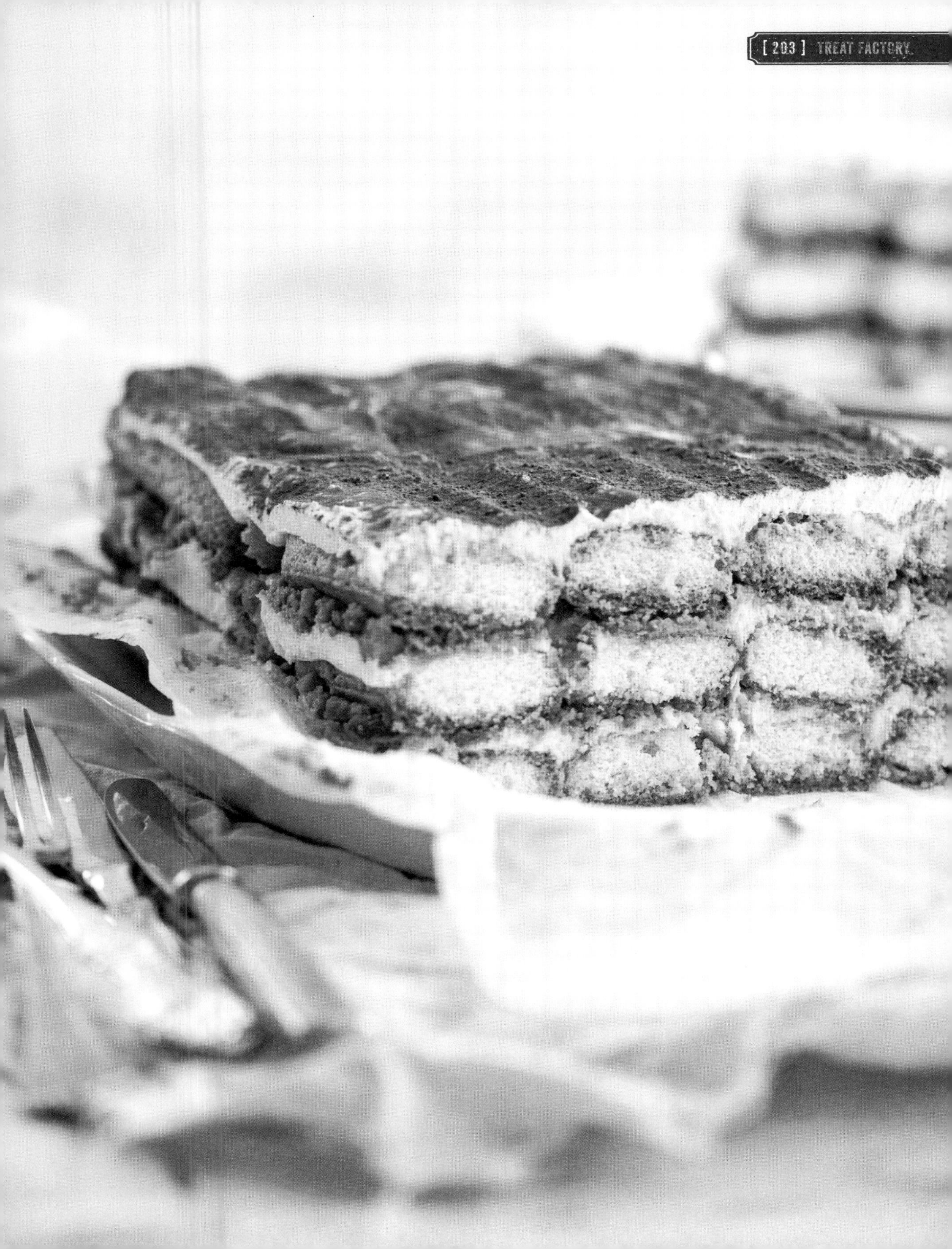

CHAI SPICED
APPLE CRUMBLE

SERVES 8-10

FILLING

450G APPLES, PEELED, CORED AND CUT INTO 1CM PIECES

4 CLOVES

½ STAR ANISE POD

1 TEASPOON GROUND CINNAMON

½ TEASPOON GROUND CARDAMOM

¼ TEASPOON GROUND GINGER

60G BROWN SUGAR

1 TABLESPOON PLAIN FLOUR

1 TABLESPOON LEMON JUICE

CRUMBLE

2 CUPS (300G) PLAIN FLOUR, SIFTED

¼ TEASPOON GROUND NUTMEG

A PINCH OF SALT

160G BROWN SUGAR

200G UNSALTED BUTTER, SOFTENED

CLOTTED CREAM OR VANILLA ICE-CREAM, TO SERVE

Preheat the oven to 180°C. Grease a 23cm ovenproof frying pan or dish with butter.

To make the filling, place the apple into a large bowl. Place the spices into a mortar and grind to a fine powder with the pestle. Sprinkle the apple with the spice mixture, sugar, flour and lemon juice. Mix well with a spoon and set aside while you make the crumble.

To make the crumble, sift the flour, nutmeg and salt into a large bowl. Stir in the sugar. Take a little butter at a time and rub into the flour and sugar mixture. Keep rubbing until all the butter is used up and the mixture resembles breadcrumbs.

Spoon the fruit mixture into the prepared pan, and sprinkle the crumble on top. Bake for 30–40 minutes, or until the top is golden.

Serve warm with clotted cream or vanilla ice-cream.

★ ★ ★

To make a gluten-free version, substitute almond meal or hazelnut flour for the plain flour.

NO CHURN
BROWN BREAD & RUM
ICE-CREAM

- 1 CUP (250ML) MILK
- ⅔ CUP (145G) CASTER SUGAR
- 4 EGG YOLKS
- 5 SLICES WHOLEMEAL BREAD (CRUSTS ON)
- 2 TABLESPOONS DARK RUM
- FINELY GRATED ZEST OF HALF AN ORANGE
- 2½ CUPS (625ML) CREAM

Put the milk and sugar in a saucepan over medium heat. Stir until sugar dissolves and milk is about to boil. Remove from the heat. Cool slightly.

Whisk the egg yolks in a large bowl. Whisking constantly, gradually add the warm milk mixture until combined. Transfer the mixture to a clean saucepan. Cook over low heat for about 10 minutes, stirring constantly, until the mixture thickens and coats the back of the spoon. Make sure it doesn't boil or it will curdle. Set aside to cool.

Tear the bread into pieces, and place in a food processor. Process in bursts until coarse crumbs form. Stir the breadcrumbs, rum and orange zest into the custard. Cover and refrigerate until cold.

Beat the cream in a large bowl until it forms soft peaks. Fold the cream into the cold custard. Pour into a metal container, cover with cling wrap and freeze for at least 6 hours. Place in the fridge for about 20 minutes to soften slightly before serving.

Do not use dry breadcrumbs or the ice-cream will not set. Stir constantly or else the mixture will stick to the pan and burn. Cool milk mixture to just warm before adding the egg or you will end up with scrambled egg custard.

CARAMELISED FIG
KULFI

SERVES 6

Kulfi is an Indian dessert. It's an ice-cream made with milk and cream, simmered with spices and reduced to caramel perfection. This caramelised fig ice-cream is a happy marriage of those gorgeous spice flavours. And the best thing is that it can be made with dried figs!

110G DRIED FIGS, FINELY CHOPPED

1 CUP (200G) BROWN SUGAR

1½ CUPS (375ML) MILK

375ML CAN EVAPORATED MILK

½ TEASPOON GROUND CARDAMOM

1 TEASPOON VANILLA EXTRACT

1 TABLESPOON MAPLE SYRUP

1 TABLESPOON CHOPPED ALMONDS

PINCH OF SALT

Place the figs and half the brown sugar into a saucepan and cook on low heat, stirring occasionally, until the sugar has melted and the mixture looks caramelised. Add the milk, evaporated milk, remaining sugar, cardamom, vanilla, maple syrup, almonds and salt.

Cook, uncovered, on low heat for about 50 minutes, until creamy and thickened slightly. Stir occasionally to make sure the mixture doesn't stick and burn. Remove from the heat and cool completely.

Pour the mixture into six ½ cup (125ml) capacity icy-pole or metal dariole moulds. Cover and freeze for at least 6 hours, or overnight, before serving.

To serve, remove from the freezer and hold the moulds under hot water for a few seconds to loosen the kulfis. Turn out onto serving plates.

CARAMEL YOGHURT
FRUIT SALAD

SERVES 4

3 CUPS (840G) GREEK YOGHURT

½ CUP (100G) BROWN SUGAR

1 LARGE GREEN APPLE, CORED AND DICED

2 SMALL BANANAS, SLICED

250G STRAWBERRIES, HULLED AND QUARTERED

3 FRESH FIGS, CHOPPED

HANDFUL OF BLUEBERRIES

Place a sieve over a large bowl (with plenty of clearance under the sieve). Line the sieve with two layers of muslin cloth (or cheesecloth). Scoop the yoghurt into the cloth. Gather the ends and twist together to form a pouch.

Place a heavy weight on top (like a mortar or a plate topped with a couple of 400g cans). Set aside to drain in a cool corner of your kitchen (or the fridge on a warm day) for 4 hours.

Scrape the drained yoghurt into a large bowl. Add all the other ingredients and mix well. Refrigerate overnight, or for at least 4 hours, before serving.

★ ★ ★

Shrikhand is a drained yoghurt dessert sweetened with honey and studded with nuts. This modern version is even more delicious with its creamy caramel tones and fresh fruit in every mouthful. Feel free to add in nuts and chocolate chips to provide more texture.

Frozen yoghurt is the new rage among serious dessert lovers. I have tried many unusual flavours, such as watermelon, taro, matcha and blood orange, but coconut is my absolute favourite. This simple recipe makes stunning coconut fro-yo at home. It only needs to freeze for a few hours after churning. The draining of yoghurt is essential to the creaminess (see page 210 for instructions). If you don't have an ice-cream churner, just mix it and chill it in the fridge for an appealing non-frozen yoghurt treat.

COCONUT
FROZEN YOGHURT

SERVES 8

1KG GREEK YOGHURT, DRAINED FOR 4 HOURS

½ CUP (110G) CASTER SUGAR

1 CUP (250ML) COCONUT MILK

Place all ingredients into a large bowl. Using a wire whisk, whisk until smooth.

Scrape into the bowl of an ice-cream maker and churn according to the manufacturer's instructions. Transfer to an airtight container and chill for 4–6 hours before serving.

Place in the fridge for about 20 minutes to soften slightly before serving.

MANGO LASSI
GRANITA

500G FROZEN MANGO

1 CUP (280G) GREEK YOGHURT

HANDFUL OF MINT LEAVES

PINCH OF SALT

FEW STRANDS OF SAFFRON

¼ CUP (55G) RAW SUGAR

½ CUP (125ML) MILK

Place all the ingredients into the jug of a blender. Process until smooth and creamy.

Pour the mango mixture in a shallow 4 cup (1 litre) capacity tin. Cover with cling wrap and freeze for 4 hours.

Remove from the freezer and scrape the frozen mix with a fork. Return to the freezer for another 4 hours.

When ready to serve, scrape granita with a fork into little wine glasses. Serve immediately.

★ ★ ★

PASSIONFRUIT BUTTER

150G BUTTER

100G RAW SUGAR

PULP OF 5 LARGE PASSIONFRUIT

JUICE OF HALF A LEMON

¼ TEASPOON SALT

5 EGGS, LIGHTLY BEATEN

Stir the butter and sugar in a heavy-bottomed (or enamel) saucepan on low heat, until the sugar has dissolved. Add the passionfruit pulp, lemon juice and salt. Mix well.

Add the eggs to the passionfruit mixture and increase the heat to medium-low. Whisk with a wire whisk for a few minutes, until combined and smooth. Change to a wooden spoon and keep stirring and cooking for about 8 minutes, until the mixture becomes thick and coats the back of the spoon – it should be the consistency of thick custard.

Remove from the heat. Spoon into lidded jars, seal tightly and store in the fridge for up to two weeks.

If you are lucky enough to have freshly laid eggs, you will find the sizes vary. This may affect the consistency of your passionfruit butter. If your mixture is too runny (it slides off your spoon easily), whisk in another egg and add a tablespoon of butter. This helps thicken the mixture to the desired consistency.

CUSTARD THICKSHAKES
WITH CRUNCHY CARNIVAL COOKIES

COOKIES

¾ CUP (115G) PLAIN FLOUR

1 CUP (90G) ROLLED OATS

½ CUP (45G) DESICCATED COCONUT

¼ CUP (10G) RICE BUBBLES

½ CUP (80G) SALTED PEANUTS, COARSELY CHOPPED

⅔ CUP (135G) BROWN SUGAR

125G BUTTER, SOFTENED

1 TABLESPOON HONEY

1 TABLESPOON GOLDEN SYRUP

½ TEASPOON BICARBONATE OF SODA

THICKSHAKE

1 CUP (250ML) BOUGHT POURING CUSTARD

2 SCOOPS OF VANILLA ICE-CREAM

1 CUP (250ML) MILK

EXTRA VANILLA ICE-CREAM, TO SERVE

CHOCOLATE SAUCE, TO SERVE

To make the cookies, preheat oven to 170°C. Grease two baking trays and line with baking paper. Combine the flour, oats, coconut, Rice Bubbles, peanuts and sugar in a bowl. Mix well.

Place the butter, honey and golden syrup in a saucepan. Stir over low heat until the butter melts. Remove from heat. Combine bicarbonate of soda with 1 tablespoon boiling water in a small bowl and add to the butter mixture. Stir to combine (it will foam up).

Pour the butter mixture over the dry ingredients and mix together. Roll tablespoons of the mixture into balls and place onto the prepared tray, leaving at least 4cm around each cookie to allow it to spread. Flatten each cookie gently with your fingertips.

Bake for 15–20 minutes, until the cookies are golden brown around the edges. Remove from the oven and cool slightly on the tray before transferring to a wire rack to cool completely.

For the thickshake, place the custard, ice-cream and milk into a blender. Process until smooth and thick. Pour into glasses and top each glass with a scoop of extra vanilla ice-cream, a crumbled cookie and a drizzle of chocolate sauce. Serve with extra cookies.

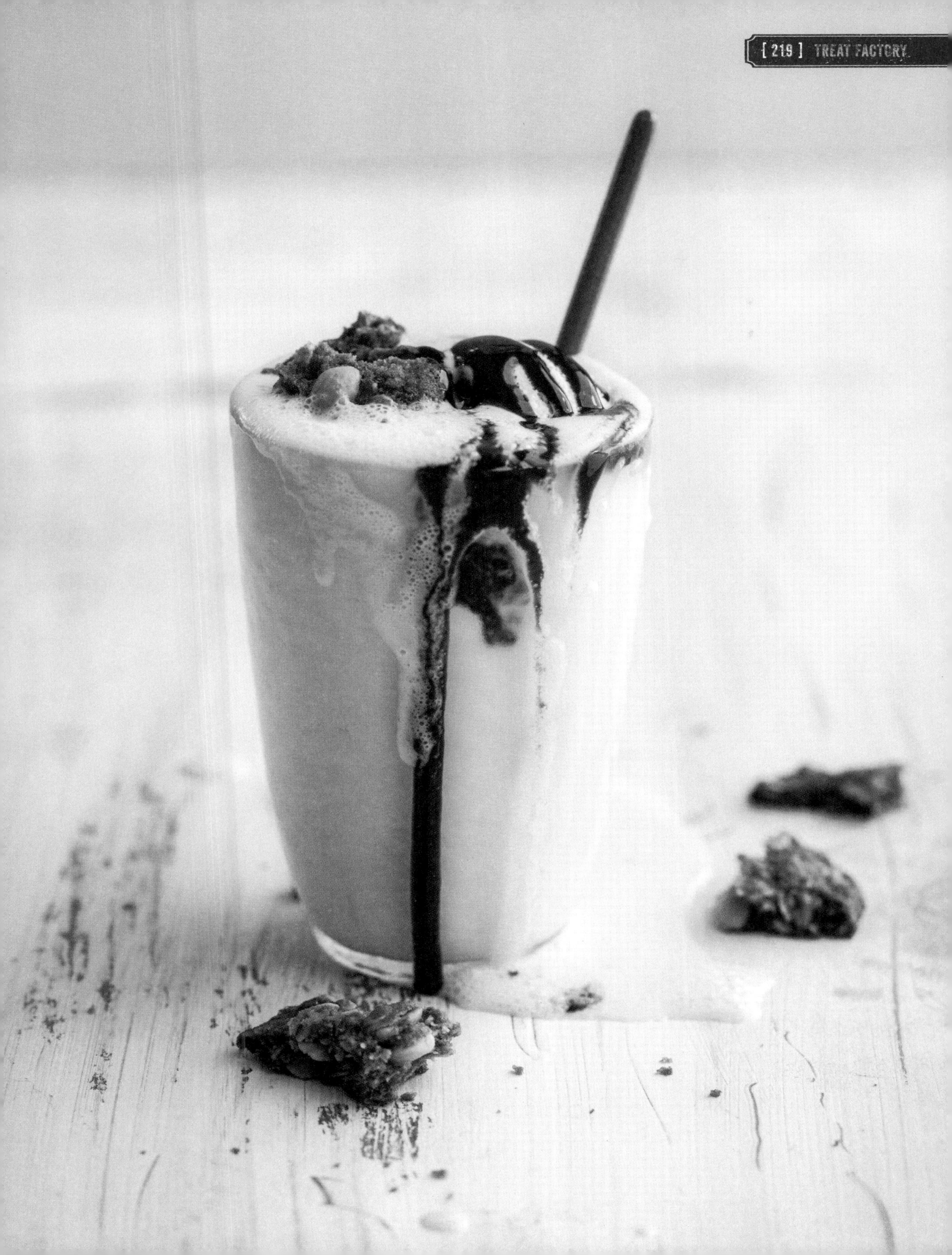

NAUGHTIES

1. ONE MINUTE COCONUT MUG CAKE

SERVES 1

4 TABLESPOONS SELF-RAISING FLOUR

2 TABLESPOONS DESICCATED COCONUT

1 TABLESPOON RAW SUGAR

3 TABLESPOONS COCONUT MILK

1 TABLESPOON LIGHT OLIVE OIL

1 EGG

2 TABLESPOONS LEMON CURD

EXTRA LEMON CURD AND CREAM, TO SERVE

Place the flour, coconut and sugar into a 1½ cup (375ml) capacity mug, and mix well. Add the coconut milk, olive oil and egg. Mix well with a spoon until smooth and evenly combined. Gently stir through the lemon curd – do not mix it completely.

Microwave the mug cake on high for 50–60 seconds, until it puffs and rises to the top, watching to make sure it doesn't spill over. Enjoy straight away, topped with extra lemon curd and fresh cream.

★ ★ ★

2. WHITE CHOCOLATE & COCONUT TRUFFLES

MAKES 20

180G WHITE CHOCOLATE BITS
(OR WHITE COOKING CHOCOLATE BROKEN
INTO PIECES)

½ CUP (125ML) CREAM

1 TEASPOON VANILLA EXTRACT

1 CUP (80G) SHREDDED COCONUT

1 CUP (90G) DESICCATED COCONUT

EXTRA DESICCATED COCONUT, TO ROLL

Combine the chocolate and cream in a heavy-bottomed saucepan over low heat. Stir constantly for 2–3 minutes, until the chocolate is melted and blended with the cream. Add the vanilla extract and remove from heat. Cool slightly.

Add the shredded and desiccated coconut and mix well. Transfer to a bowl and chill, uncovered, for at least 45 minutes, or until the mixture is firm enough to roll into balls.

Roll tablespoons of the mixture gently into balls. Roll the balls in extra desiccated coconut or in crushed nuts for a delicious crunch. Refrigerate until time to serve.

★ ★ ★

3. ROAST STRAWBERRY & CINNAMON SAUCE

MAKES 1 CUP

350G STRAWBERRIES, WASHED, TRIMMED AND QUARTERED

2 TABLESPOONS MAPLE SYRUP

1 TABLESPOON LIGHT OLIVE OIL

1 TABLESPOON BALSAMIC VINEGAR

1 TEASPOON VANILLA EXTRACT

1 TEASPOON LEMON JUICE

½ TEASPOON GROUND CINNAMON

¼ TEASPOON SALT

Preheat the oven to 180°C. Line a rimmed baking tray with baking paper. The rim is important to prevent juices from spilling during roasting.

Place the strawberries into a bowl. Add all the other ingredients and mix well. Spread evenly onto the prepared baking tray.

Roast for 30–40 minutes, until the mixture is sticky and has a jam-like consistency. Remove from the oven and cool slightly. Store in a lidded glass jar in the fridge for up to a week.

★ ★ ★

ACKNOWLEDGEMENTS

Writing Tasty Express *has been like being on the proverbial rollercoaster – without the safety belt on and juggling 10 plates stacked with food in each hand! It's been an exhilarating, totally wicked ride. The book was conceptualised and created in a one-room studio and each recipe was tested and cooked on a three-metre steel bench with portable cooking equipment and a really old oven. But it has been an unforgettable experience and it was made possible by many good people with big hearts and large appetites helping me create something special and tangible.*

Nick, you always believed in me and knew long before I did that I would write this cookbook. You were my rock, my constant in a room full of ingredients, props and photographic equipment. You washed up, ran errands and let me have an occasional tantrum. You gave this book the most perfect name I could have wished for. Thank you for your incredible love and for always being there for me.

Rivvy and Rishi, my sweet little boys, your encouragement and excitement (especially at having your own pictures in a book!) are a joy to watch.

Mum, you gave me the gift of cooking. Without you I would never have known what I love so much in my life. Dad, you taught me possibly the most delicious way of cooking chicken. Rushil, you have always been the most enthusiastic recipe tester. Thank you!

Jill, this book became a reality because of your vision and foresight. Thank you for seeing something that nobody else had and believing in me enough to pursue it with me. Nikki, I am grateful for your leap of faith and for the opportunity you gave me. Trisha, you were amazingly patient in dealing with me! Thank you for creating something so beautiful from my constantly evolving ideas. Kate, the advice to 'just breathe' was what I needed on some days. Thank you for that. And thank you to everyone at Random House for their awesome support!

Petra, it was such a joy working with you each day of the shooting – cooking, knocking back ideas, taking lots of tea breaks and powering through the shots. You were the most fabulous assistant/friend I could have asked for. Petra, Julie, Esther – thank you for being the sisters I never had.

Minh, Tim, Tanya, Clare, my classmates and the gang at Shillington, you inspired and supported me through a crazy time and allowed me the time I needed to make it happen. Thank you!

Thanks Hayden Quinn and the Monday Morning Cooking Club girls for coming through for me. I truly appreciate it.

Thank you Jamie Oliver – you are my food hero!

And finally to all my blog readers, fellow bloggers and social media buddies, I could dream this dream because of you. Thank you for following my journey from start to finish. Thank you for your amazing love!

INDEX

An Ebury Press book
Published by Random House Australia Pty Ltd
Level 3, 100 Pacific Highway, North Sydney NSW 2060
www.randomhouse.com.au

First published by Ebury Press in 2014

Addresses for companies within the Random House Group
can be found at www.randomhouse.com.au/offices

National Library of Australia
Cataloguing-in-Publication entry (pbk)
Roy, Sney, author.
Tasty Express / Sney Roy.
ISBN 978 0 85798 352 7 (paperback)
Cooking.

641.5

Cover and internal design by Trisha Garner and Sneh Roy
Recipe writing, art direction and styling by Sneh Roy
Project food editing by Tracy Rutherford
Recipe preparation by Sneh Roy and Petra Holland
Index by Puddingburn Publishing Services
Printed and bound in China by Everbest Printing Co Ltd

Random House Australia uses papers that are natural,
renewable and recyclable products and made from wood
grown in sustainable forests. The logging and manufacturing
processes are expected to conform to the environmental
regulations of the country of origin.